# MY
# NON-
# IDENTICAL
# TWIN

# MY
# NON-
# IDENTICAL
# TWIN

## Evie Meg

SPHERE

SPHERE

First published in Great Britain in 2021 by Sphere
This paperback edition published by Sphere in 2022

1 2 3 4 5 6 7 8 9 10

A CIP catalogue record for this book
is available from the British Library.

ISBN 978-0-7515-8407-3

Printed and bound in Great Britain by
Clays Ltd, Elcograf S.p.A.

Papers used by Sphere are from well-managed forests
and other responsible sources.

Sphere
An imprint of
Little, Brown Book Group
Carmelite House
50 Victoria Embankment
London EC4Y 0DZ

An Hachette UK Company
www.hachette.co.uk

www.littlebrown.co.uk

**For anyone who's ever felt alone**

# Hello!

Hi! My name is Evie Meg. I was born on 22 July 2000. Nice to meet you!

First of all, thank you so much for picking up my book, I really hope you enjoy reading this and maybe learn something too. I am so excited to have this opportunity to share my story with so many people, and hopefully to inspire others who may be similar to me to open up and seek support. For those of you who can't directly relate to my illnesses, I hope I can open your mind to people who may be a little different and show you what it's like living with a disability – the good and the bad. I hope by sharing what's happened in my life so far, I can help you – whoever you are, whatever you're going through – to feel positive about life and know that every storm comes with a rainbow!

I've written this book during the last few months of 2020 and the beginning of 2021, while the world has been going through a global pandemic. I hope whenever you're reading it that the crisis might be over. In any case, I don't think many people can say they wrote a book during that time, so I am proud to have done so. Since we were all stuck indoors and the shops and colleges were closed, I have had plenty of time to sit and write this book and brainstorm ideas. And let me tell you, when you read a book, you don't think of all the effort that's gone into writing it; you just sit back and enjoy the story. I'll never read books the same way again!

Some of you may know me as 'This Trippy Hippie', which is my online name. I am lucky enough to have a large platform online, which I use to spread awareness of a condition I live with that affects my daily life: Tourette's syndrome. If you follow me already, you're definitely going to learn a lot more about me than what's on social media. If you haven't met me before, it's so nice to meet you! I'm excited for you all to get to know me and my condition better; I really hope you love my book.

You may be wondering, what does 'My Nonidentical Twin' have to do with Tourette's? Often when my Tourette's is bad, it doesn't feel like me. It feels like I am a puppet attached to strings and someone is pulling the strings and making me move and say things. Or like I am being controlled by a remote and someone is just pressing a load of random buttons. I see my Tourette's as a naughty character that's always with me wherever I go. I choose to describe it as a 'nonidentical twin' because it looks like me from the outside when I jerk and make strange noises, but on the inside it's not me.

If you don't know what Tourette's is, or have a vague idea but want to know more, don't worry, I'm going to teach you everything I know by taking you on a journey through my life story so far. Tourette's affects my life every day, but I've had to contend with some other, very challenging illnesses too. I pride myself on being a positive, happy person so I promise I'll be holding your hand all the way, but there are a few darker patches that might be upsetting, so make sure wherever you're reading this you're looking after yourself.

Maybe under a snuggly blanket or with a dog on your lap or biscuits by your side.

Are you sitting comfortably? Then let's begin!

# Welcome to the Family!

I live in a lovely detached red brick house in a town in the north of England and I'm writing this book at my desk by the window. You can picture me surrounded by many, many plants – they make my heart happy just by looking at them – and lots of crystals, which bring me peace. I'm a big believer in making your room your safe space. My room is one of my favourite places to be, because everything in it is a little bit of who I am as a person.

On practically every surface are candles and lights and hanging from the ceiling are my dreamcatchers. I also have beautiful wall tapestries. One has a giant realistic-looking African elephant on it, which for some reason I named Sheila! They complete my room and make it cosy. On the bed is Lottie, one of our cats, sleeping soundly.

If you were here on a pre-Covid-19 Sunday, I'd take you downstairs to our dining room for a roast dinner. It would be so delicious that the smell would hit you before you opened the door. And, don't worry, my mum and I are vegetarians so if you don't eat meat there'd be a tasty option for you, too.

Round the table would be my mum Sam, my dad Iain, my two brothers Joshua and Daniel, and my grandma Maggie, who is great at baking and who lives just around the corner – our back gardens are only separated by a fence. It's lovely living so near to her!

I am incredibly lucky to come from such an amazing family, and I am very grateful for how close I am to all of them. Me and my parents couldn't really get any closer. We've got on well all my life, but I think my disabilities and mental health difficulties over the years have definitely strengthened what we already had.

My parents met when Mum started working at National Savings – Dad had already been working there for quite a while. She was eighteen, he was twenty-five. At first Mum thought his job was to do everyone's photocopying but turns out he would just jump up and do hers anytime she went near! They started dating and quickly became inseparable, marrying a couple of years later. When I was really unwell, my mum actually left her job to take care of me – by that point she was a teaching assistant in a primary school. I felt awful, because she had been working there for years and I know that people there loved her. She really is an amazing woman.

Because she left her job, we were at home together 24/7. We did absolutely everything together, and through my struggles we became even closer and our bond is unbreakable. I really don't know what I'd do without her.

My dad is a lovely man, a lifelong Newcastle United supporter and huge Beatles fan! He calls me Migmogs. He has driven me to countless appointments, therapy sessions and to hospital when I've needed it. I'd have been stuck without him, and I wouldn't have been able to get the help I needed. Both of my parents care for me so well when I am poorly and I am so grateful for all that they have done for me. I know that I must drive them a bit mad sometimes, especially when my Tourette's is being mischievous! But they never get angry; they have always accepted me as I am.

My older brother Joshua is a very gentle and chilled person. He is a huge bookworm and enjoys walking. He's always popping his head round the door and saying, 'I'm going for a wander!' Mostly, he heads off by himself – I don't often go with him in case I have any kind of episode. I wouldn't want to put him in that position. Mum and Dad are the ones who usually deal with any incidents. Besides, he walks too fast and I can't keep up!

Daniel, the youngest of us three, is also very chill! He can seem shy to strangers but with family, he can be a bit of a chatterbox.

Growing up with two boys wasn't all bad, and I don't mind being the middle child. Joshua was born first, he's twenty-three at the time I'm writing this. I was born three years after him, and another three years later Daniel came along. Joshua and I were both born in hospital, but Daniel was born at home. I still remember some of it; it was close to Christmas and Joshua and I were watching Scooby-Doo together in another room while Mum was giving birth in her and Dad's bedroom!

I did wish I had a sister to share my love of dolls and teddies with, though. My mum has three brothers, so she knows what it's like being the only girl. Luckily, I had lots of cousins growing up and I'm quite close to my cousin Libby. We had some pretty big fights when we were younger – it's hilarious to think back to those arguments because they were basically over nothing but we would get so upset! For example, when I was staying in her home for a while, Libby became very jealous that I was playing with her younger brother more than her. She started a huge fight and slammed a door in my face! But mostly we got on famously. We both absolutely loved *High School Musical*, and we had matching HSM T-shirts with our names on. I remember we once went to a restaurant wearing them and I proudly paraded us around, hoping people would look at us and think, 'Wow, look at those twins!'

Not round the table for Sunday lunch, but who I ordinarily see lots of, are my grandma Isabel and grandad Bill, who are my dad's parents. I have a real soft spot for all my grandparents, I love them to pieces. Grandma Isabel, like Grandma Maggie, is a great baker; we get a big cake once a week. She's also talented at knitting –when I was in primary school, she made me beautiful red cardigans that had cute strawberry or ladybird buttons. During this awful time of coronavirus, Grandma Isabel has knitted over 200 tiny hats for newborns, to donate to the local special care baby unit to provide a bit of warmth for premature or poorly babies. Isn't that amazing? They are so cute, in so many different colours, and she has said she will continue making them for as long as this lockdown lasts, and possibly after.

The last time I was there I stood in the doorway of their little bungalow and looked through this huge carrier bag of tiny woolly hats. 'You're amazing, Grandma,' I said to her while admiring all the work and time she has spent selflessly knitting to help others.

She replied: 'Oh, not as amazing as you, sweetheart.'

My grandad Bill is the kindest man you'll ever meet. And

very handsome, if I do say so myself. He is also one of my biggest fans. He bought himself a T-shirt which had 'This Trippy Hippie's Grandad' printed on it! I was smiling so much when he showed me a photo of him wearing it for the first time. He plans to wear it to a tennis tournament to show it off.

Grandma Isabel and Grandad Bill have been married for sixty years now and counting. They are a great couple and they do make me laugh.

'I haven't found my Prince Charming yet,' Grandma Isabel joked to me once down the phone.

'He's sitting right here,' came Grandad Bill's voice and I could hear them both chuckling to themselves.

My grandad Edwin, Maggie's husband, sadly passed away in 2008 after battling cancer. He was an incredible artist; he did amazing paintings and even made us all glass clocks. I wish he was still here. I do lots of art myself so I'd love to show my pieces to him and get some tips. He was a lovely man.

My heart bursts for my grandparents, I really couldn't love them any more than I do. The support they give me means the world.

Sorry that I can't provide you with an actual Sunday lunch, but, to be honest, I can be a bit of a tricky dinner companion anyway because my naughty nonidentical twin can make me throw things, stab down my cutlery and interrupt conversations! She hasn't always been around, though. She first came into my life when I was about twelve, and none of us recognised her for who she was when she first appeared. Let me take you back to the very beginning.

# My Childhood

**Me as a child – written by Mum:**

Evie arrived into the world three days early and screaming her lungs out! It wasn't a particularly difficult birth. At one stage there was mention of a Caesarean section because of her heart rate dropping low but then the labour proceeded quickly and she arrived without needing any help.

The first thing that I noticed was her huge blue eyes and ridiculously long eyelashes! They were so long that some had tucked themselves back up under her eyelids and had to be pulled out. She seemed quite angry to have been disturbed and cried for ages, only stopping with many renditions of 'Twinkle, Twinkle, Little Star'.

She was an easy, sunny baby who always watched her big brother Joshua with great interest. As she got older they were great friends and played together well (most of the time). Joshua was a huge Scooby-Doo fan so lots of their games revolved around Scooby-Doo and the gang, and being chased by monsters.

Playing restaurants was a big favourite too. They would get all the plastic toy food out, create a menu, then ask us to come to their restaurant. They were very happy kids, Joshua laid-back with a wicked sense of humour, Evie sassy, determined and a bundle of sunshine. Three years after Evie arrived, her younger brother Daniel was born. He was due on Christmas Day and I decided very early on in the pregnancy that I didn't want to be away from my kids at Christmas and planned a home birth. Daniel was luckily born a few days early, on 22 December, at home. Evie very quickly became a little mother hen to her baby brother.

I loved playing with Daniel. We were both obsessed with Sylvanian Families (mostly me, though!). Mum would some-times clear the dining room for us so that we had enough space to make a whole village for all the shops and the ani-mals to walk around. I especially loved the bakery. It had a spinning mill outside it and inside were tiny loaves of bread, biscuits, and even little jars of jam. I also collected Blue Noses, which were soft toys of different kinds of animals which all had blue noses and little patches on their sides. I ended up with at least twenty-five!

Another of my other many collections was Jacqueline Wilson books. I've never been a big reader, I always found it a little boring, which feels a bit wrong to say when I'm writing my own book! Jacqueline Wilson's books were the only ones I was drawn to. I adored her cosy and friendly style of writing.

One of my earliest memories is about one day at nursery, so I must have been about three years old. I was playing in the water tray with some friends. We were all wearing little plastic aprons so we didn't get our clothes wet. I remember there being yellow ducks bobbing around.

While I had a happy childhood, my health was never exactly plain sailing, and it was around my third birthday that I started to be unwell, with high temperatures and periods of intense shivering. My mum had me backwards and forwards to the doctors for weeks. I had loads of tests but just kept getting worse until I was finally admitted to hospital on a paediatric ward.

They finally found the source of infection. It was in my kidneys, one of them was defective, splashing urine back up into my bladder instead of expelling it, meaning I was getting recurring urine infections. I needed strong antibiotics for quite a while after that.

During my stay in the hospital, I was rushed to the paediatric cardiology unit. I was so small that I didn't understand those words at the time, but it was soon explained to me that they had discovered I had a heart murmur. This came as quite a surprise to my family, as no one had heard it before!

The murmur was found to be caused by a small hole in one of the valves in my heart, meaning that blood was leaking back into one of the heart chambers. It was tiny and not causing any problems with my overall health, at least at first. I had to start going for check-ups at the hospital every two years, which felt very boring when I was little, but I had no clue as to what lay in store later. The real issues with my heart only started in the summer of 2019.

I began having these strange short episodes of heart flutters. (Not the technical term!) They are incredibly difficult to describe, almost like my heart gets hot. I know that sounds bizarre but it's really hard to find words to describe the feeling. They usually only last a couple of seconds, and we weren't sure if they were caused by anxiety, like palpitations. My mum and I decided to bring them up during my next appointment, just in case they were something more serious. I'm glad we did because it's definitely not caused by anxiety!

This appointment was very different to the ones I was used to – they usually tell me the hole hasn't changed and that everything is totally fine. This time, though, I did get a bit of a scare . . .

The cardiologist explained that the flutter episodes were caused by my heart defect, and told me and my parents that if the episodes begin to go on longer than ten seconds, I will need keyhole surgery. This was a massive shock, but he said that it could be way in the future, or may not happen at all.

Walking out of the hospital, none of us knew what to say, until my dad broke the tension. 'Well, that was intense, wasn't it!' He was right, that was not what we were expecting at all.

There is no pattern to my heart flutters whatsoever – they happen any time, any place; some days I have none and some days I'll have seven.

Annoyingly, having a heart defect means I've always been told by my cardiologist that I mustn't have tattoos or piercings (oops!). Okay, so I have a few piercings ... I know that was naughty. I love to express myself through the way I look, and my piercings are a part of that. I will never get a tattoo, though. Getting a tattoo with a heart defect is a lot more dangerous than getting a piercing, so as much as I'd love a few tattoos, I have to keep myself safe.

When I thought there might still be a chance of having one, I designed myself a simple flower. I would love to have it on my arm. I'd also love a tiny moon on my wrist, to represent me and my mum. We have a special song and the lyrics include 'baby to the moon and back, I still love you more than that'.

I'm a mandala artist (more on that later!), so I would also love one of my own mandala tattoos, too. I guess I'll have to keep dreaming. But at least I can stick to temporary tattoos.

My first ever best friend was a girl named Hannah, who was in my reception class. She had really cute curly hair, and we had something in common. Even though we were little, we could relate to each other, because she had a heart defect too. Hannah's was worse than mine at the time, and she had surgery when she was only five. I remember she came back to school and showed me her scar. Hannah and I became very close; we were always together for the short time that we knew each other.

A couple years later she moved back to Malta and I haven't seen her since, but she always has a special place in my heart. We follow each other on social media so we can still keep up to date with what we are doing. She has grown up to be so beautiful.

Luckily, when I was five, a lifelong friend came along at Christmas. I have always adored Christmas. The decorations, all the different colours on the tree, the smell of yummy food, all of it. I especially love cosying up on the sofa with blankets and chocolate and watching my favourite Christmas films – these include *Elf*, *Home Alone* and *Miracle on 34th Street*. Nothing better to get your Christmas spirits up!

That year I came excitedly downstairs on Christmas Day and something really stood out to me: a beautiful sunflower bag sitting among the presents. When I opened it, inside was a lovely brown bear with a red ribbon tied in a bow around his neck. He was really gorgeous; his fur was so shiny and soft and he had a lovely face. I fell in love with him pretty quickly. In the bag there was also a card, which had a lovely drawing of a bear on the front, which looked a lot like my new bear! The card read:

To Evie,

Hello. My name is Popcorn. Father Christmas has sent me to you because you asked for a bear you could write to.

I love to write letters and draw pictures. I hope we will be best friends and you will love me very much.

Love from

Popcorn x

I was so over the moon. I had received lovely presents that year but he was my favourite. From then onwards, I began to write him letters and draw him pictures. At the beginning I often just gave him scribbles because I was so young, but I would leave the picture on his lap while I went to school, and when I got back he would have replied!

My parents had actually been quite sneaky. At that time, my writing skills weren't where they should have been. I was falling behind a bit, so they thought if they got me a bear who liked to draw pictures and write, it would encourage me to do the same and I would improve. It worked! My reception class teacher saw a big difference in my handwriting and spelling skills.

I would sometimes leave Popcorn a small bowl of honey while I went to school, and when I returned it was smudged on his nose! I remember the feeling of being at school and wondering if he had replied to my letter or eaten his breakfast. It really did feel magical, I'm so glad my parents did it for me. I definitely plan to with my future children.

For years we wrote letters back and forth; he would wish me good luck for any tests I had or ask if he could watch TV with me, and I loved it so much. He really felt like a friend.

When I was around ten years old, I started to have some doubts. This may seem late for me to realise, but I have always been quite young at heart. I sucked my thumb way past the age that most people do – it actually pushed my front teeth forwards and I had one thumb skinnier than the other!

I wrote Popcorn some letters asking if he really was real, or if my parents wrote the letters. When I discovered it wasn't actually him that drew those pictures or wrote those letters, of course I was disappointed, but I never stopped loving him. He always came with me for every holiday or trip we went on. He was never, ever left behind.

And as I grew older and my health declined, he came with me for many, many hospital trips, comforting me as I lay in a hospital bed feeling fed up. I always felt so much safer there when I had him with me. He no longer looks like he did all those years ago, his fur is all curled and flat, and he is very skinny, but he's still one of the most precious things in my room.

Discounting Popcorn, my oldest best friend is a girl called Eve. We became close, at the age of six, when we were in year 2 of primary school together. I went to a fairly small primary, only around 200 pupils. It was a lovely school, though, so colourful, and all the staff were so nice and friendly. When I first started there, I was definitely one of the smallest. I had short curly brown hair and a fringe.

I was good in school; I was never causing trouble. In fact, I got in more trouble for not contributing during lessons than for actually being naughty. Which seems funny because now, if I went into a classroom environment, my naughty nonidentical twin and I would be incredibly noisy and disruptive!

One of my strongest memories is probably because it was at odds with my shyness. I was playing on the climbing frame and I decided to challenge myself and climb on top of the wooden monkey bars instead of using them how you're supposed to. I climbed up and got myself stuck because I was too frightened to move. I told someone near me to go and get the lunchtime supervisor, and they came over and had to carry me down. They were smiling quite a lot; they must have found it funny. At the time I was so tiny that those monkey bars looked as tall as a house. Now they'd probably only come up to my shoulder.

Eve is such a sweet person. She had a lovely smile and fine hair, we just instantly clicked. We became best friends very quickly, and soon we were literally joined at the hip. I'm not joking when I say that we didn't really have many other friends; we only needed each other. I had a few others, but it was always Eve I would look for and wanted to be with. As we moved up in primary school, we were very rarely seen one without the other. I remember one lunchtime we were in the toilets and another pupil came in, saw us and said, 'Are you two sisters?' I can't remember if we said no or just went along with the idea!

Me and Eve have never had a fight. (Well, we had a tiny one in year 4 over a pencil, and we didn't speak to each other for a whole afternoon. Which was the longest we had ever gone without talking to each other.) So far we have been best friends for around fourteen years, and I know for a fact that Eve is a friend for life. Which was good, because when we went to secondary school I really needed her . . .

# Corridors and Competitions

My time at secondary school (which for anyone reading this outside of the UK is school for kids aged eleven to sixteen) isn't very nice to think about, but it's not something I'm going to forget in a hurry. The first couple of years were decent, although it was a big change. I felt so tiny – I hadn't really grown much and I was one of the smallest in my year – and the school was much bigger than I was used to. There were three floors, and the place was so big the teachers gave us a map to help us find our way around (this made no difference to me because I really struggle to read maps!).

I found the timetable quite difficult, and like any typical year 7 pupil I was often late for my lessons at first because I just couldn't find the classroom. Luckily, because it happened to so many of us, we didn't get into too much trouble.

In other ways, life was good. When I first started secondary school, I was in love with gymnastics and doing really well at it. I was three when my parents put me in a gymnastics class. Of course it wasn't proper gymnastics, it was more like jumping around and rolling on the floor, but everyone's got to start somewhere! My dad created folders of photos, leaflets and certificates throughout my time doing gymnastics, and the first thing in the folder is a certificate from 2003: I had just come out of hospital after the problem with my kidneys when my parents took me to a class. I was so excited to get started.

As time went on, my gymnastic skills improved. I was lucky because I had a natural flexibility that just came easily to me. (I hate sounding like I'm bragging, but I really was lucky to have a naturally bendy spine.)

When I was eight, I won my first ever medal – it was only my second competition. It was a simple floor routine – nothing too complicated – but at that age it felt like the Olympics! I placed second and I was over the moon, though I look so terrified and awkward standing on the podium in the videos and pictures; I was so shy that my neck had shrunk into my shoulders. The feeling, though, was amazing. I was always terrified of climbing the podium in case I tripped or something, but once you were up there and the judges managed to place the medal around your neck (it would often get caught on the tight buns we had on our heads), 'Simply the Best' would play loudly over the speakers and everyone would clap for a minute or so. I still remember that feeling.

The same year, I took part in my first Christmas display. These were shows that the whole club performed every year, usually five nights in a row, from around 17 December to the 22nd. I was in one routine, 'The Ugly Bug Ball'. I was dressed as a greenfly, in a green leotard, with green pipe cleaners wrapped around my buns as antennas. I also had floaty material attached to my arms and leotard as mini wings. My face was also painted green, with round yellow cheeks. I was nervous, but I loved it – rainbow lights, which were set up all around the two big bouncy gymnastics floors, would shine down as we performed. In later years there were even smoke machines! It was just a great time to have fun and perform. It could be so tiring, though. I remember going to school with glitter in my hair every day, then coming home and going for another night of displays. I definitely didn't feel like an 'ugly bug', though. I just felt amazing.

Not long after this, I found my first real gymnastics friend. A blonde girl called Rachel. We had the same sense of humour, and just giggled until we almost wet ourselves all the time. We ended up in the same group from ages ten to sixteen so at first we found it tricky to train hard without glancing at each other and starting to chuckle!

The Christmas display 2010, when I was ten, was my first ever display in a trio, as a top. Before, I'd been practising with the other younger kids in the back rooms, but now I was training on the actual gymnastics floors! Gosh, I remember how nervous I was, suddenly feeling so exposed and on display. And being in a trio meant we did acrobatics together – I remember being so nervous to work with them, and it was nerve-racking at first putting so much trust into someone that they won't drop you! At this time I was also scared of heights, so it was a little scary climbing up people and being thrown around. There was one move – years down the line when I was at a higher level – where the bases would do a handstand with their feet together (I know it's hard to picture but bear with me!) and I would climb up them and perform a handstand on their feet. I was at least five feet off the ground, which doesn't sound too bad, but balancing on other people's feet, doing a handstand, while everything wobbles, to me was terrifying. Being in a handstand, of course, you're forced to look down, and it made me feel sick. So I would try to then jump off halfway through the move.

One session I even came in wearing my 'lucky socks', which had hedgehogs on them, and I was hoping I'd somehow be able to do it, but of course I was still so scared of this particular move. Every session, as we built up to it, I could feel the anxiety rising, and the same thing happened every time – I'd get up there, begin to go into a handstand but then jump off. I was told off so much by my coach for this, which at the time upset me; I even shed a few tears on the gym floor once. But I know now that she was only angry because she knew I was capable. 'Tough love' I think is the name for it!

Going back to the beginning – I soon became good friends with my first ever partners, and we became pretty hopeless because we just giggled constantly. Sometimes I'd run and jump and they'd catch me on my belly and we would just crumble because we were laughing so much. We were only at beginner level, doing very basic trio moves, but I can fully understand why we got told off a lot.

I wasn't in this particular trio for very long, only a few months (I wonder why!). It was when I was in my next group that things moved up a notch. We worked so hard, and my gymnastics timetable was changed from one evening a week to four, and training three-hour sessions at a time. This was a big change, but I was young and fit so I was up for the challenge.

The ultimate goal was to get to the NDP (National Development Program) finals, the British Championships, but first you had to win regionals to qualify to go there. Our first real try was in March 2011. We were given a special new routine. The music was upbeat, and some parts of the choreography were quite fast. Even though this was ten years ago, I still remember pretty much all of the choreography for this routine, and to this day, even after all the others, this one still remains my favourite.

I remember the car journey travelling to the competition so clearly: Dad in the driver's seat, Mum in the front passenger's seat and me in the back. We put music on to try to distract me but the sickly butterflies in my stomach were overwhelming. I knew nerves were a good thing, though, and that I could use them in my performance.

We arrived in our gym club tracksuits. I always felt a sense of pride when I walked around wearing mine; it's such a great feeling to be part of a team doing something you love. I'll never forget all the hairpins, bun nets, and the strong smell of hairspray! I took a packed lunch since we would be there all day, and for some reason it became a thing for me to have Tic Tacs in my lunchbox every competition I went to. We had to be careful we didn't eat or drink much before our routine, though, otherwise we could be bloated or it could make us feel sick and heavy.

When it got closer to the time of our routine, all the trios in that category got roughly ten minutes to go on to the floor and warm up. This was not always a good thing because if we messed up a move in the warm-up, it really set off our nerves for the real thing. But that day we did it all perfectly.

After the warm-up finished, we sat on the gymnastics floor opposite, watching the other trios and waiting for our turn. I can't even describe how nerve-racking this was. It was so tense watching the others go on before us, because if they were great, it was a bit unsettling. I coped with nerves a lot better when I was this age though; it didn't bother me as much as it would when I went into my teens.

When the trio in front of us was coming towards the end

of their routine, we put chalk on our hands to give us better grip and walked to the edge of the floor. We were in our leotards by this point, of course. They were beautiful, a shiny red with a flame-like diamanté pattern all over the front.

The trio before us walked off, and, as our names were called, we walked on to the floor in sync, presented ourselves to the judges, and got into our routine starting positions. Then we had to wait for the 'beep' to let us know the music was about to start.

My starting position was down on my knees with my hands by my side and my head down. I remember so clearly looking down at my thighs, taking a deep breath, preparing myself to start. I watched the diamanté on my leotard sparkle on my belly as I inhaled and exhaled in the silence.

Then, the music started and it was go, go, go. There was no time to be nervous now as we needed to be focused on trying our hardest and remembering everything our coaches told us.

At this time, the music accompanying gymnastics routines wasn't allowed to include lyrics, so it was all beats, drums, guitar, any instrument really! Our dance matched up with the beats of the song so it flowed nicely and looked effective.

Thankfully, during the routine I was so focused and moving all the time that my nerves disappeared. However, when holding a move for three seconds, I just thought, 'Please don't fall, please don't fall!'

I remember the feeling of relief when I knew we were near the end of the routine, and that we hadn't made any mistakes! It was an amazing feeling to know we got through it all with no errors or falls.

That routine saw us take first place, which meant … we

were through to the NDP finals! This was a pretty big deal since it was my first time going to the nationals, and I felt both amazing and terrified at the same time. But my parents came running over to give me the biggest hug, and I was so excited in that moment.

The British Championships were only two months away, so we trained hard to perfect our moves and the routine. For the British, we had to travel further, about three hours for us in the car. This wasn't like the regionals; we actually had to stay at a hotel overnight before competing the next day. I loved this but it felt like it dragged out my nerves.

We stayed in a Premier Inn, and near the hotel was a cute street with lots of shops. One of them was a Charlie Bear shop. I've loved teddies since I was little, but all the ones in this shop were so posh! I loved looking around all the different coloured bears with different fur textures and facial expressions. They had so many, there were even some going up the walls. Even though they were expensive, I was so entranced by them that Mum told me if my trio got a gold medal she would buy me a Charlie Bear. I was so excited, and knew I'd need to give it everything I had.

And that's just what we did! We became British champions for the first time! I was so proud of us. As we walked up to the podium, we shook hands with the trios in second and third place. I always found this super-awkward and worried whether my hands were really sweaty and sticky! On the podium we were given a single flower, a rose, and the medal in a case with an engraving of the year.

And, of course, I got my Charlie Bear! I picked a small bear that had lovely shiny dark brown fur, and I named him Champion. I still have him, and he's in great condition, sat happily in my room with Popcorn. In fact, around this time I owned a Nintendo DS, and when I look through the camera roll on it, there're about twenty photos of me and Champion that I took in my bedroom one evening! They're pretty hilarious.

Less than a month after the British Championships, in early June 2011, there was an article in the local newspaper about me and my trio. They included a photo of us in our lovely red leotards, holding our rose and medals, which was taken the day of the competition. The article read:

'The trio fought off 12 teams to be crowned Champions last month, despite the fact it was the first time they have competed together in a major competition.

It's Evie's first year competing, the other two girls have been to the British, but for them to win it shows they have potential.'

I asked my coach, Katie, if she'd write something about that time. This is what she said:

*I've had the privilege of coaching many gymnasts over the years but I will always remember Evie. When I think back on her time as a gymnast, I have many fond memories. I remember her competing in a red leotard in the regional qualifiers at a gym in South Tyneside. It was such a proud moment to watch Evie and her partners complete an almost flawless routine and go on to qualify for national finals with one of the highest scores of the event. The three girls went on to national finals, where they competed against the other finalists from across Britain. The competition was tough. I knew they were good but it would take something special to*

*win. The girls performed with such style and*
*confidence and proceeded to take the gold medal.*
*Despite her success, Evie was always incredibly*
*modest and humble.*

So, yeah, when I started secondary school in 2011 I was actually a British champion! It's something I'm so proud of when I look back at it and I think it's important for me to hold on to that sense of achievement, because it proves that people with disabilities can be really good at things. But it was during this period of time that my life changed for ever, in various different ways. Let's start with Tourette's.

# And so it Begins...

I was around twelve or thirteen years old, and Eve and I were at school. We were just hanging around the corridors when I began hiccuping.

'You've got hiccups again?!' Eve said, smiling.

She was right, and actually I'd had hiccups all weekend. In fact, I couldn't remember the last time I hadn't had hiccups! We wouldn't learn the truth for years – that this was a tic caused by my Tourette's.

I even went to the doctor's after I'd been hiccuping daily for months, but they didn't know what was causing them. We thought maybe something was wrong with my diaphragm so I tried eating slower. Of course this didn't work at all because they weren't real hiccups. So every day for (literally!) years, I was 'hiccuping' up to a hundred times, including in the classroom and in assemblies.

My 'hiccups' actually became an in-joke with me and Eve. We laughed about them all the time, wondering how on earth I still had daily hiccups after so long. We were young at this stage and I hadn't even heard of Tourette's before and had no clue what a tic was, either. Of course, me and Eve were so shocked when years later we found out these strange constant 'hiccup' noises were actually part of a neurological condition which would later massively escalate and affect my daily life.

## What is Tourette's Syndrome?

Now for the sciencey bit – are you ready? Tourette's syndrome is a neurological condition where the signals in our brains misfire and cause involuntary movements and sounds – these are called tics. Physiologically, there's a section at the back of our brain called the 'basal ganglia', which is connected to our spines and controls our motor function. In individuals with Tourette's syndrome, the basal ganglia are malfunctioning, causing uncontrolled movements and vocalisations. These tics usually start in childhood, between the ages of two and sixteen. However, in some rarer cases, there can be an adult onset, usually caused by trauma or maybe a head injury.

There are many, many different types of tics; some are simple and some are complex. Simple tic examples would be sniffing, blinking, nose scrunching, throat clearing, grunting sounds, etc. Complex tics include repeating words or phrases, saying something in a different tone of voice or accent, jumping, hand flapping, biting, etc. Tics are also put into two categories: motor and vocal tics. Motor tics are any that involve the body, whereas vocal tics are of course any using the voice box.

Tourette's syndrome is a spectrum, so no two people with

TS are the same. Some, like me, say words, full sentences, while others may not have any word tics, they may only make noises like coughing, whistling and humming. This does not, however, make their case of Tourette's less valid. Tourette's is a hard thing to live with, no matter what type or how many tics you have.

**The different tics have different names:**

There's the compulsion to repeat other people's words or phrases. This tic is called **echolalia**. I have this tic quite frequently – it's a bizarre feeling. I can try to hold myself back but it gets uncomfortable and eventually I have to repeat what's been said and in the exact same tone of voice the person used. It sometimes happens when I'm at the shop checkout; for example, if the cashier says, 'That's £9.99 please' or 'Would you like a bag?' I'll often feel a strong urge to repeat their words, which can seem to them like I am mocking them, but I simply cannot control it.

There's also **echopraxia**, which is a tic where we involuntarily mimic other people's movements. I remember one day Mum and I were walking down our local high street, and a man came walking towards us carrying shopping bags in both hands. He had a sort of swagger in his walk, and my Tourette's started mimicking him. I held both arms out as if I was carrying heavy shopping bags and my shoulders went back and forth. I was so embarrassed as he walked past us! Goodness knows what he must have thought.

**Palilalia** is a tic in which we repeat our own words. Personally, my palilalia isn't great, and people online who watch my videos often ask if I have a stammer as well as TS, when in fact the stammering is a tic.

Another type of tic called **copropraxia** means involuntary obscene gestures, for example 'giving the finger' (this is a tic I do daily!). Not everyone with Tourette's has all of these; it varies from person to person. Are you still with me? Brilliant, now it's time to tackle the most infamous of all . . .

## The F*#k!@g Swearing Tic

Probably the most well-known thing about TS is the sudden swearing. The actual name for these tics is **coprolalia**, and despite the common belief that having Tourette's just means swearing uncontrollably, actually only one in ten people with TS swears. Unfortunately, I am one of them!

It is thought that coprolalia is caused by damage to the amygdala, which is the section of the brain that controls anger and aggression. This is the scientific thinking behind it, however when we swear we are not usually angry or aggressive at all!

There's a huge stigma around Tourette's that all we do is shout awful words and swear all day. It's not true. We often have hundreds of tics, but the coprolalia is the most eye-catching and the most memorable, so it stands out to everyone more than just the twitches.

# Tourette's – There's More Than Meets the Eye

What a lot of people don't realise is that there's a lot more to Tourette's than what you can see on the outside. You can see us twitching, jerking, making noises or saying things, but you can't see internal tics.

Believe it or not, some individuals with Tourette's have tics that happen only in our minds – these are called **mental tics**. Mental tics can happen at any time and can be extremely annoying. You may be wondering 'how on earth does that work?', so let me explain.

Mental tics fall into the category of 'skepsi' tics:

There's **echoskepsi**, which is just like echolalia, except we don't say it out loud. So, for instance, with echolalia I used the example of me repeating 'Would you like a bag?' after the lady at the checkout said it to me and my mum. However, with echoskepsi, this is when I would involuntarily repeat something I've heard over and over in my head. So instead of saying it out loud, it's replaying in my head.

**Coproskepsi** is like coprolalia, but again, it's us repeating swear words over and over in our heads, and this is totally out of control.

**Paliskepsi** is the one I personally struggle with the most. This is the mental version of palilalia, involuntarily repeating our own words in our heads.

Mental tics may seem okay because at least we are not saying things out loud, but in a way they may be more of a nuisance. We can't just 'release' the words the same way we can when they come out of our mouths.

In Tourette's syndrome there is a sensation that some of us have which is called a 'premonitory urge'. This is the build-up feeling that we experience in our bodies before a tic happens. With outside tics, this premonitory urge can usually be 'relieved' by movement. Whereas with mental tics, it's a lot harder to 'satisfy' that itch. For me at least!

My mental tics rarely happen during the day, but when I'm trying to sleep they go nuts. It's not the same as 'over-thinking'!! As I lie in bed trying to fall asleep, my brain will start repeating random words over and over again, and it's so hard to get it to stop. Not so long ago I was lying with my eyes closed and I was really comfy, but I couldn't stop repeating the word 'compromise' in my head. I mean, why that word?! It's not exactly something I say a lot. And the sentence, 'Do you like it? Do you?' I have no idea why but I couldn't stop it from playing in my head – it's like an internal broken record. In case you're wondering, my nonidentical twin, I don't like it, so let me sleep now please!

As bizarre as it sounds, it's so frustrating for anyone who experiences mental tics and they do keep me awake at night.

My first ever mental tic was when I was really young – I think it actually started before my tics visibly appeared. Before every single thought in my head, I would say 'hash-tag'. Weird, right?

'Hashtag I wonder if we're nearly home.'

'Hashtag I need the toilet.'

Just like that. It wasn't constant, but when the tic came, it hung around for long periods at a time. I wish I could say it helped me in my future social media career, but all it did was annoy me for months on end. It even affected song lyrics, so if I had a particular song stuck in my head, it wouldn't be playing normally, it had 'hashtag' before every sentence. It was totally out of my control and it took me a while to notice it was even happening.

You might be wondering how I got Tourette's. Well, the truth is, the cause of TS is unknown. However, it is thought that you're born with the genetic predisposition and it just doesn't develop till later, possibly due to environmental factors. Sometimes it develops out of nowhere, sometimes it is triggered by trauma or a head injury. For everyone with Tourette's, their tics will develop at different times. For some, their tics appear when they are toddlers, and start as maybe rapid blinking or small jerks. Whereas for others, like me, the tics start in their early teens. But it wouldn't be for years that I would actually know that what was happening to me was Tourette's.

In the meantime, another illness was becoming far more debilitating. Around 85 per cent of individuals with Tourette's syndrome have more than just their tics. So many of us have other disorders as well. These are called 'comorbidities' – when you have more than one condition present at the same time. The most common comorbid conditions that go hand in hand with Tourette's are OCD (Obsessive Compulsive Disorder), ADHD (Attention Deficit Hyperactivity Disorder) and anxiety. And, boy, was I hit with this last one.

# Starting to Struggle

When I was in year 9, so aged thirteen and fourteen, my mental health started to really decline.

I hadn't had too much of a problem with school in years 7 and 8. Eve came to the same secondary school as me, which was a huge relief for the both of us, because I was so worried we were going to be separated. We even ended up in the same form class, so I loved seeing her then for a short time before we went off to separate lessons.

Me and Eve are very different academically. We have spoken about this now we are older, but when I was younger I struggled with it. Eve is really smart, she always did well in her classes and is awesome at playing the flute. I was never exactly jealous of her, I was of course proud of her, but I did wish that I was a little bit brighter, because when we started secondary school, we were put in different 'sets' based on our abilities. This meant that Eve and I had many classes where we were apart, and it was so strange being away from her at first. I actually had to talk to other people!

Even though I was a curious kid, I always knew that I was never going to be top of the class academically. For example, all my life I've struggled with numbers and maths. This was clear from an early age, and in year 2 (age six to seven) I was tested for dyscalculia, which is dyslexia but with numbers. So for years I was in the bottom set for maths. In primary school I was in a separate group, for pupils who needed a bit of extra help. Yet I was good at English, and because of my gymnastics I was good at things in PE like hurdling and long jump.

I didn't like being in the lowest class, especially since at secondary school, we had to line up outside the classroom waiting for the teacher to let us in. I wanted to hide my face so people didn't see me.

Teachers didn't always make school easier, either! I was in a French lesson once when I started to really need the toilet. I asked the teacher but she said no. I literally crossed my legs I was so desperate. I sat there for ages because I didn't want to annoy the teacher when she had said no, but I kid you not, I thought I was going to wet myself in the middle of French class. I stuck my hand up and waved it around frantically; she saw me, I asked again and told her I really needed to go. She said, 'Yes, quickly', which was fine by me because I certainly needed to get there quickly! I hated using the school toilets so I very rarely did, but this time I didn't really have a choice. I'm not joking when I say I ran down the corridor. I mean, I actually ran. It was more like a sprint. You know how important it is to look 'cool' in secondary school, and I never wanted to make myself look like a fool, but this time I really did. You'll be glad to know I just about made it in time.

Another toilet story in case you were eager for more: I was in an IT class when I started to need a wee. (It sounds like

I have some sort of bladder issue but I promise I don't!) So I put my hand up. This alone was a scary thing for me because it made me really nervous. I asked the teacher if I could go to the toilet, and I don't remember exactly how she reacted at first, but afterwards she said, 'You've got two minutes, any longer and you'll have detention.'

I was quite surprised by this and contemplated just holding it in, but I didn't want a repeat of French class, so I hurried out the door. I remember thinking to myself, 'Oh, this will be easy, there's some toilets just round the corner', but when I got there that corridor was sectioned off because of older students doing exams.

I tried pacing over to another corridor further away, but by the time I got there it had already been at least two minutes. I sort of just fidgeted about a bit then turned around and went back to IT as fast as I could. I felt like a right numpty, and I still needed the toilet. I got back to class and said to my friend next to me, 'I didn't even go!' Of course they laughed at me but I wasn't happy.

I asked my mum what she remembers from that time. This is what she said:

> When Evie started secondary school we weren't worried. Despite being tiny and a bit quiet we knew she had all her friends from primary school with her and her elder brother was at the same school and enjoyed it.
>
> The first couple of years passed without much incident but when Evie was fourteen things began to change . . .

This was because that 'shyness' escalated into full-on social anxiety. I started noticing I was becoming more 'shy' when I began feeling unsafe at school. I wasn't being bullied or anything like that, there was no one person making me feel unsafe, I just did. I hated walking around the crowded corridors, people bumping into me, all the noise of everyone talking at once. I really, really hated it. It made me feel so overwhelmed and like too many senses were being over-loaded at once. I started feeling too anxious to eat in front of people, so some lunchtimes I would just have a drink and not eat till I got home.

I also began really struggling with assemblies. I didn't like these from the start, because I disliked the layout of the school hall. It had stairs with seats on an uphill angle, and we had to walk in front of everyone in the silence to sit down with our form group. I was so scared of everyone staring at me and judging me, and later on, when I talked to my therapist about it so we could work through it, they explained that it was anxiety telling me this, and if I looked around I would see that no one was actually staring at me, they were busy focusing on themselves.

So I tried this, and I know that usually it really is a false intrusive thought, but on this occasion it was totally true, everyone stared at whoever came through the doors. I strug-gled with this massively, and as I got more and more unwell over the years there, I started having panic attacks at the doors of the hall.

One morning in year 10, I had arrived at school a little late. I was already shaken up before going through the school doors because I knew it was assembly day. By year 10 I was really poorly with my mental health, and I saw that everyone was already sitting down in the hall. I panicked so much thinking about walking in front of 300 students all by myself.

I couldn't go in. I sat down out the way and started crying. My breathing wasn't great, either. My head of year, who by this time knew I was struggling, came over, sat opposite me and said, 'Having a bad day?' I nodded and he took me to one of his lessons. I sat quietly by myself in the classroom until assembly was over. I was so embarrassed; the pupils in the class were older than me, and my face was red and puffy from the panic attack.

This is so strange – imagine how younger me would have felt if she knew all her struggles and experiences were later going to be written in her own book!

One of the saddest things is that this anxiety had also trickled over into my gymnastics. Not long after we became British champions for the first time, I broke my arm badly in a training session and had to have pins put in it. I was unlucky and it was a very messy break. But I was desperate to get back to training as soon as it was better, and nine months later my trio and I were back at the regionals, and then on to the nationals – where we won again! We'd become British champions for a second time!

But after that, some of the joy started to go out of it. I became upset at gym more often, got frustrated with myself when my fear of heights held me back from performing higher-skilled moves which I was actually capable of doing. And my trio started to move and change around.

I made a big decision to quit gym. My mum messaged Katie and told her the news. She was shocked and upset and asked us to meet with her. So one day Mum and I went into a back room at the gym and sat down with Katie. I was absolutely dreading this; I didn't want to go. However, I'm so glad I did. Katie actually cried a bit! She suggested that I come back to gym, as a base. So I would no longer be thrown around or balancing on top of people – I would be on the bottom, throwing someone else around!

So that's what I did. I came back as a base and I was so much happier. I loved being a top and switching to a base is totally different. I did miss feeling like I was flying, and being on top doing the complicated moves I was proud of, but I was excited to see what the next chapter in my gymnastics story had in store for me.

I was put into another trio, and the other base was a friend I had known for a while, Jenny. I was really looking forward to this. Jenny is such a lovely person; I miss training with her and hearing her laugh. She was so strong and muscly which made her a great base.

We were given a new top, a girl I had never seen before. She was so tiny but she was lovely and together we competed several times.

But inch by inch, my anxiety started to claw its way into my performances. I felt so riddled with anxiety that I just wasn't myself when I performed anymore. I began wearing leggings and jumpers so that my whole body was covered up in training. Obviously, for gymnastics this isn't ideal at all but I did it for years. I remember looking round and seeing that I was the only gymnast wearing leggings and with my body fully covered.

I started having panic attacks during the sessions; I would take myself into the toilets and hide. One session some of us were given a pretty white leotard to try on for a Christmas display routine, 'Fields of Gold'. It had shimmery silver patterns on top of the white and attached were white floaty nets, which almost looked like angel wings. I thought it was so delicate and pretty, but I hadn't had so much of my body on show for such a long time that I went into the toilets, put on the leotard and didn't come out of the cubicle. I convinced myself I looked awful, and I felt so anxious I just sat on the toilet and cried. My lovely coach Katie came to check if I was all right, since everyone else was out except me.

'Evie?' a voice came from outside my cubicle. 'Are you okay?'

I knew it was Katie, which made my nerves worse. I didn't want her to see me like this.

When I finally emerged, Katie and my other coach Vicki sat in a room with me for a bit while I calmed down. They told me I looked lovely in the leotard and I tried to slow my breathing down.

The 'Fields of Gold' routine was beautiful, and I also had a routine with another girl – a duet where we performed graceful flexible moves. I loved having a time to shine but it made my anxiety so bad. Most of the performances I managed, but on one of the nights, I had a panic attack. I was hyperventilating in the toilets again and I completely missed the whole routine. No one knew where I was. Mum found me and helped me calm down but I still missed the routine. The girl I did the duet with had to perform it on her own.

I asked Mum if she'd write a bit about what she remembers from that time. This is what she said:

> At first we noticed an anxiety at
> gymnastics that hadn't been there
> before. Evie still loved gym but was

worried about people looking at her and judging her. Then her friends at school began to worry too. Evie was not joining in with conversations anymore. She would sit with her head down, blocking out the noise and commotion around her. She was throwing her lunch away because she was too socially anxious to eat in front of anyone. The light behind her eyes changed, they were dull and sad. It was as if someone had switched off the joy. Her smiles weren't as real and she began to have meltdowns after school.

Sometimes my head of year at school would take me aside to his office so we could chat and he could find out how I was doing. This could happen during lesson time, so when I had to go back to class, it meant I had to walk through the door by myself and find my seat in front of the whole class. I know this isn't the end of the world, but at the time it felt like a huge deal.

I found this extremely difficult. I often stood outside the door for a while trying to find the courage to just open the door and go in. It got me so worked up, I usually ended up going to the toilet till the end of the lesson and just pretending I was with my head of year the whole time.

Then, my head of year decided it would be a good idea to refer me to CAMHS (Children and Adults Mental Health Services) which is a mental health service in the UK. It was there that I was diagnosed with social anxiety. It was nice to talk to someone about all my fears at school, but it felt painfully awkward.

My head of year also arranged for me to leave lessons a couple of minutes early, to avoid the stress of rush-hour traffic in the corridors. This helped a lot, and it did reduce tension in that area.

I kept my issues pretty secret from my friends. In fact, the one person I found it the hardest to tell was Eve. This wasn't at all because I thought she wouldn't understand, because of course she would. I think it was just harder because I had known her the longest and loved her the most. I didn't want to burden her.

Which I now know is ridiculous. I can't stress enough how important it is to open up to people; they would want to know if you're suffering mentally and it feels so good to have the weight lifted off your shoulders. You don't need to carry that around by yourself. Let someone help you.

By the time I was fifteen, things were getting even worse. I began some really self-destructive behaviours and depression set in.

It's so hard to think about, let alone write in a book for the world to read. But I'm choosing to share this because I know how many students struggle at school, and I want them to know that they are not alone.

I started having this overwhelming sadness that just didn't go away. At times it was numbing, and I didn't feel a thing. At those moments I hid in the toilets, just because I needed somewhere to cry in private. It really was a dark time, and I'm not going to include every detail in this book, but I also want to be as honest as I can be.

My head was an awful place to be. Concentrating in lessons became a really big task. I remember one lesson I had my head down trying to write but the page was all blurry because I was fighting back tears. I had so many people around me, and many friends, but I felt so alone. That's no one's fault; it's just the cruelty of depression.

> Evie's teachers were telling us she was working well but was very quiet and wouldn't speak up about problems or when she didn't understand something.
>    She started to ask to stay home, she was finding it too difficult to go to school. She felt unsafe in the corridors, unsafe in class. The noise at school, the social interactions, the drama was all too chaotic and overwhelming.

An event that stands out in my mind happened one afternoon at school during a PE lesson. I was quite late because I had been helping a friend who'd become unwell during a lesson with me. I went into the changing rooms by myself and started to change into my PE kit. The changing rooms were completely empty because everyone was in the gym hall. I noticed when I was almost finished changing that I'd become very shaky and wobbly. My breathing started speeding up, so I sat down on one of the benches. My legs were shaking and I couldn't control it.

I was in such a state that I barely noticed my friend had come in until I heard her say, 'Evie, you okay?'

I just crumbled. I burst into tears and went into a full panic attack. She sat with me and tried to help but the panic attack only got worse and I couldn't speak. She went to tell a teacher and soon all my friends heard what was happening and I was suddenly surrounded by people. The teachers came in and tried to find out what was wrong, but the hyperventilating was so bad I couldn't get a word out. I was taken to a first-aider and a quiet room to calm down. I felt so rotten when the attack ended; my head hurt and I was exhausted.

As my problems progressed, I started trying different medications, like antidepressants. Medication for mental health is quite a controversial topic – some people don't agree with it and that's fine. I respect that, but I was not opposed to taking pills, and I was willing to try anything that might make me feel better.

It was very much a case of trial and error: one medication turned me into a complete zombie, and made my depression a lot worse. I didn't find the right medication until after leaving secondary school. You're lucky if you find the medication that suits you on the first try, so don't lose hope if a particular one's not right for you.

Asking around and seeing what medications other people have tried isn't a bad idea; however, every single person reacts differently. So, for example, the medication I'm on now is the perfect one for me. Yet for someone else, it may have made their depression worse, or had other effects. And the ones that didn't work for me may have been perfect for someone else.

It's also important to know that medication isn't a quick fix. You also have to do some of the work! The medication may ease your symptoms, but you have to do the important stuff. Like not giving up, and pushing through it all. I hate to be a cliché, but it really does get better. I am proof of that.

I'm guilty of once believing that it never gets better. That life would always feel that dark and that I was never going to stop feeling the sadness hanging over me. Man, was I wrong.

What a lot of people don't realise, or just don't think about, is that while mental health is a psychiatric problem, it can also have a lot of physical effects on the body. When I started to feel more anxious in school, I always felt it in my chest. Some people feel it in their stomach, but I always felt like my heart got hot whenever I was anxious. Like the feeling when your heart sinks if you miss a step going down the stairs.

In year 10, when it all got worse, the physical symptoms got worse too. Stress can have a big impact on your body. My hair started to fall out, and I had noticeable bald patches on the side of my head which I covered up with a bandana or headband.

During GCSEs and mock exams, I became so stressed that I got shingles. Shingles is a viral infection – it's basically an adult version of chicken pox. Me and Mum noticed rashes along my belly and hips. They were itchy and painful. I was still allowed to go to school, because as long as no one touched the blisters – which I kept covered in dressings anyway – the virus could not be passed on. My mum had to speak to the school about dress code, because the waistbands on the skirts and trousers were so painful on my shingles. So they allowed me to wear a skintight black dress with my school shirt and blazer on top, which was good because it just looked like I had a tight skirt on so I don't think anyone really noticed.

I did stay off school for a day or so at first because I felt quite ill, but when it settled down I went back in for my exams. I remember sitting in the giant exam hall trying to concentrate but the rashes were so itchy.

Another physical effect the stress caused was migraines. I used to have the most awful migraines, some so bad that I couldn't lie down, so if I tried to sleep it off I had to sleep sitting up. Luckily, before an attack I got a warning sign, so this gave me time to prepare and get to a dark place or take paracetamol. The warning is something called an aura, which usually involves disturbances in vision. A lot of people have different auras, some have tunnel vision, or maybe blurriness.

Mine was strange, and I've never heard it talked about before. My vision was drastically impaired, to the point where I almost went blind on one side.

One of the earliest yet worst migraines that I remember started when me and my parents were shopping in TK Maxx back in 2013. I specifically recall that we were in the bedding section, when suddenly my vision became halved. By that I mean, if I looked at my mum's left eye, the right side of her face would just disappear. Yet if I looked over at her right eye then the same would happen to the left side of her face, it would just be darkness on one side.

The same when looking at a sign. If I read a sign that said 'Migraine', obviously I'd start at the 'M', so while looking at the 'M' I would be able to read 'Migr-', and if I shifted my focus to the rest of the word, I would only be able to see '-aine'. I couldn't see the whole thing at once. Does that make sense? It was horrible but at least it let me know about an attack in advance.

I was terrified when it happened in the shop, it was a horrific feeling. I told my parents straight away and they took me home.

I was given some strong emergency medication for my migraines, which was kept at reception in my secondary school. I couldn't take them too often because they were powerful and addictive, but they did help.

With my depression getting worse and worse, I could no longer cope with all the lessons I had, and five lessons a day for an hour at a time. History was one subject I especially struggled with – there were so many things to remember, and my head was already so full of destructive thoughts that I couldn't retain a thing. I just zoned out for an hour instead of taking part. So my head of year agreed to cut history out of my timetable.

I was doing art GCSE at this time too, which was so demanding. We had a lot of work to do at home, and I was rubbish at the criteria we had to fulfil. It's funny because around the time I started my art GCSE, I began doodling more.

I started drawing just random patterns on bits of paper, often in between lessons. I can't remember if I found inspiration online, but I began drawing different patterns with details. I found out this style had a name – mandala.

A mandala is a spiritual symbol in Buddhism and Hinduism. The mandala is a circle, representing the universe and that life is never ending and that we are all conected; however it can also represent the spiritual journey of the artist. The word mandala translated in Sanskrit literally means 'circle'! Mandalas are made up of beautiful patterns and intricate designs.

I straight away found this style of drawing extremely therapeutic. I was able to just zone out and go into my own little world while drawing a mandala. The designs usually took an hour at the very least, depending on the size and detail. Some can take a few days.

But unfortunately there was no mandala GCSE and, when

doing art at school, you have to fit into a box. You can't do your own style. I would constantly compare myself to Eve, and my other friend who was so amazing at art, and their art folders looked incredible. Mine was just full of sticky notes from the teacher telling me I was doing stuff wrong. It really brought me down and made me so upset. My friends will remember, but for months I refused to let anyone look in my art folder. I ended up dropping art as well.

PE then became too much of a task. Unfortunately, depression takes away your energy levels and motivation. It felt like too much to even get out of bed on a morning, so to go to a building I was afraid of, be in loud and busy corridors and do PE was simply a step too far. I couldn't do it. The last subject I dropped was French. It felt like my world was just getting smaller and smaller.

# Animal Antics!

Right, things are getting pretty heavy, aren't they! So, before I explain what happened next, let's hit pause and talk about something comforting that could always be counted on to cheer me up when I was in my darkest days: animals!

I have been drawn to animals since I was tiny. I've been able to connect with them without even trying. Animals are such a huge part of who I am, and such a big part of my life, that I just had to write about them. If I didn't there would literally be a chapter of my life missing.

One day when I was about six or seven, we went to a farm, and at the entrance you could purchase small paper bags full of feed for the sheep and the goats. I loved this, although the sheep were quite slobbery! I was wearing a coat and a long skirt with tights underneath, and I was busy feeding the goats when I felt a tug. I looked down and realised a goat was eating my skirt! I was laughing and shouted for my mum. I pulled away but the goat was determined to have a bite of my skirt. Mum had to come over and try to make it let go. That's one of my earliest memories of having fun with animals.

I was always desperate for a pet at home. My mum and dad grew up with animals and I wanted to as well. In 2008, for my eighth birthday, I started begging my mum for a rabbit. I was only little and I now know that rabbits aren't great pets for children, but I was so desperate.

On the morning of my birthday, my parents took me into the kitchen and told me to look out the back door. On the deck in front of us was a big rectangular thing and I had no idea what it was. Something moving caught my eye. I saw a patch of fur and two gorgeous floppy ears. It was a bunny! The big rectangle was a hutch, but it took me ages to figure that out! The rabbit was just a baby, I think she was only around four months old. She was a lovely looking rabbit, mostly a caramel colour, but with some white and black patches. One thing I remember most about her was a black patch on the back of her head. For some reason, this black patch was softer than the rest of her. I loved stroking it.

Because of her colour, we named her Fudge. Not very original, I know! Owning Fudge was a bit of a whirlwind. We attached a run to her hutch so she had more room and could eat the grass. She loved being in her run, and even sat out in the snow. One winter, it snowed endlessly, and the snow ended up being a couple of feet deep. This didn't stop Fudge sitting in her run!

She was so feisty and had no problem showing off her atti-tude. She hated being picked up – my dad actually still has scars on his arms and wrists from where she put up a fight.

Fudge was my first proper animal friend, and I was determined to do a great job looking after her. Sometimes in the summer, we blocked off the garden, made sure there were no gaps under the fences, and I let Fudge run around and explore the garden. This made me so happy, to see her hopping around. She even sometimes dug a little hole and flopped on top of it so her little belly hung down in the hollow! That's one of my favourite memories of Fudge.

It was a great time when she was out; however, getting her back in was an almighty fuss. She loved being out so much that we could never get her back in her enclosure. As she hated being picked up, we couldn't really do that. Sometimes it would already be dark and we'd still be chasing her round the garden!

No matter how well you know someone, though, they can still surprise you. One day when Fudge was at the vet's, the vet told us that Fudge was actually a boy. While this was a big shock, it didn't make much difference to us as Fudge is quite a unisex name. A few years later, Fudge was at the vet's again. We were then told once more that Fudge was a girl. So we spent years not being 100 per cent certain what her (his?!) gender was, and even now I'm not quite sure.

Sometimes my dad wasn't keen on having a rabbit because she dug so many holes in her run, and it sort of made the garden look a bit scruffy. One morning, I went out to feed Fudge and couldn't find her anywhere. Her hutch wasn't massive so there was nowhere she could hide, and her run was just an open space so I would easily be able to see her. I couldn't see anywhere she might have escaped either. I was upset and went and told Mum. I was reassured that she would turn up soon. I was confused and distraught, thinking that she must have got out somehow.

Literally two days later, I saw her hopping about her run. I was thinking, 'What on earth is going on?' Again, there was no damage to her run, no gaps where she could get in or out. I just didn't understand.

Then I saw Fudge happily disappear down a hole she had dug. I then realised that for two whole days, that little sh*t had been in the ground. I couldn't help but laugh a bit, but we were worried about how deep that hole must be, for her to stay down there for so long. She must have been coming out at night to get some food or water then disappearing again for the day so we couldn't find her.

After this we decided it would be best not to have her on the grass! We put down a sheet in her run so she still had plenty of room but she couldn't dig anymore. This worked perfectly.

Fudge was such a brilliant first pet, and I have so many lovely memories of her and all the trouble she caused. I had eight amazing years with her before she passed, and she's buried in my back garden now with one of her favourite toys.

Over the years we've had a few other pets, including several hamsters, and in October 2010 we got a tortoiseshell kitten. We named him Alfie, and he was incredibly mischievous! He loved to scramble into boxes, and he even took an interest in people's ankles, grabbing them while you were walking. He became a bit of a menace . . .

His first Christmas with us was interesting. He straight away was fascinated with the Christmas tree. Even when we were putting up the fake one and it was in separate bits on the floor, he was diving into them head first and flashing his bum at us. When the trees were up, it was difficult to keep him out of them. He climbed up the trunk and he actually pulled the whole tree down one day. He was quite a hyper-active cat, and not easy to forget.

Really sadly, after only a few months, Alfie disappeared and was never found. Mum and I put up posters around the area but it didn't turn anything up. It was rubbish never knowing what had happened to him, but as the months went by it did get easier. I think most people who've had cats have had to go through something similar because of the number of cars on the road. The alternative would be to not let your cat out, but that wouldn't have suited Alfie at all.

In 2011, we decided it was time to get another kitten. We brought her home on my brother Joshua's birthday, and, because of this, she was wearing a white ribbon around her neck when she was given to us. She was a pretty black kitten with green eyes and about six individual white hairs on her chest. She was very sweet; we named her Lottie. She was timid, but had no problem exploring her new home. She settled in well, but less than a month later, we decided she was lonely and that she needed a friend. Cats don't always like the company of other cats, but Lottie was only a few weeks old, which is the perfect time to introduce a new kitten. We made sure we did it very slowly and carefully.

That's when Beano came into our lives. You remember my gymnastics coach Katie? She is a huge cat lover, and one of her fluffy ginger cats had had a litter. She said we could have a kitten, so one evening we went over to her house to choose one. The mum was absolutely gorgeous. We chose a kitten and decided on the name Beano, to suit his ginger fur.

Both cats were so, so lovely and had their own characters. They were quite different: Beano adored being outside and going on adventures, whereas Lottie likes sunbathing, eating a lot, and sleeping on my bed.

Beano was out and about almost every day. He was such a lover of the outdoors, and often went out hunting. We have a cemetery near our house, and for years it's been a great spot to just go for a quick walk to get out of the house. One spring afternoon, me, my mum and my brother Daniel had a walk down the cemetery. It was a lovely warm sunny day, and while we were there, Beano appeared. He must have been out on his usual adventures but heard our voices. He rolled around on the ground showing us all his gorgeous fluffy tummy. The sun hit his ginger fur and he looked beautiful. He walked with us for the rest of the way with his tail happily in the air and then followed us home. It was like walking a dog!

Beano often visited neighbours' houses, and they liked seeing him because he never hassled anyone, he just loved saying hello. One day we got a message from our neighbour saying they were eating their dinner and suddenly Beano was in their living room with them! He must have snuck in somewhere! He also popped next door occasionally too.

Beano was a great hunter. A little too good sometimes. As wonderful as he was, and as much as we adored him, he sometimes brought some of his 'finds' home to us as presents. He brought home birds, mice, rabbits, all sorts. I never liked it – as someone who loves animals more than anything, I found it hard to love that side of Beano. Sometimes the poor things were still alive, and we tried to save them but they were usually in shock.

Beano was a very fit and healthy cat. He had fantastic agility – he put Lottie to shame! Lottie, bless her, now struggles to even get on to my bed, but Beano could climb trees, fences – he even climbed up the ladder on Daniel's bunk bed so he could settle there for the day. He also had a little routine where he climbed up the garden fence, walked along to the gate, and from there he could jump up to the roof of our house. He walked along the roof, and sometimes he just sat on the point and looked around, but more often he would saunter all the way along to my parents' bedroom window, and climb in. My parents were often woken up in the middle of the night by Beano. He'd had a long night out hunting and exploring, so now he was up on the roof, meowing at my parents' window ready for a nap.

Lottie is my little shadow. We have had a special bond for years now. She favours my room over anyone else's and she chills with me all day, every day. I always know where to find her. Sometimes if she wakes up and I'm in the bathroom, I'll open the door and see that she was sitting waiting for me the whole time I was in there, and then we go back to my room together again. She's a beautiful cat; I'm not quite sure why she's always so tired since she never does anything, she doesn't even move that much . . .

Lottie is about nine years old at the time I am writing this; in fact, as always, she's sat behind me on my bed glaring at me, probably wondering why I'm not fussing her! If I sit on my bed and write this book on my laptop, she walks all over the keyboard so I use my desk instead.

Lottie has had a few health issues to overcome herself. When she was around six years old, we noticed a fleshy lump growing in her ear. (Gross I know – sorry!) It made her lose her balance a lot, so she was often wobbling and falling over. She had some small operations to remove the lump but it just kept growing back. Over time her balance got better, but her ear still didn't look great.

In April 2020, the lump was bigger than ever and we decided enough was enough. I knew the full operation was expensive but I couldn't let her go on any longer. I paid for the operation myself, and although this was during the start of Covid, it was classed as emergency surgery so she was seen pretty quickly.

After the surgery she was absolutely high as a kite. They managed to keep the outside of her ear, but there is nothing inside it. You can't really tell anymore when you look at it. She had a cone around her neck to stop her scratching at her stitches, which she wasn't very impressed with! Bless her, she looked so funny. She is now doing great – she's deaf in one ear but it doesn't affect her too much. I do have to be careful not to scare her when I come in my room, though!

When I was a teen and I started struggling with my mental health, Lottie and Beano were a big comfort. The days when I felt so quiet and empty, I would go searching for Beano or Lottie. Their loud purrs were enough to make me feel a bit better.

The way Lottie followed me around made me feel so loved and lovable, even when I didn't love myself. Beano was an instant mood booster. I think his beautiful warm ginger colour just made him radiate happy vibes. He was truly gorgeous. Beano sadly passed away on Mother's Day 2019, but we cared for him as best we could right until the very end. We buried him under the plum tree in our garden, which he loved to climb and watch the world from. He is a huge miss in our family.

In 2018, near my eighteenth birthday, I wanted to try owning a rabbit again. I couldn't get the thought out of my head. I was desperate for another rabbit. I talked about it constantly. I even started coming up with bunny names!

At this time we had Lottie, Beano and a tropical fish tank in my room. I've always thought that I would just care for so many animals if I could. I have a fantasy where I picture me sitting in a beautiful place, everything around me is so green. Plants with giant vibrant leaves, waterfalls, big flowers, and I'm surrounded by animals. Sounds like bliss. I just want to keep them all safe from sickness and abuse. Animals are family, even the wild ones. Throughout the years I've had many animals, and I could never see myself without at least one in my home for the rest of my life.

Knowing what a rough time I was having during college, my parents gave in and finally allowed me to get a bunny. We went to the pet shop to pick one out. Me and my parents had already done a lot of research so that we could do things even better this time. We read that rabbits prefer being in pairs, and my mum surprised me in the shop and told me I was getting two! I couldn't stop smiling.

I picked out two bunnies that were sisters, Lola and Pip. Lola was a beautiful all-white rabbit with pretty blue eyes. Pip was an unusual colour. She looked like two rabbits in one. Her face, head, neck and one of her front feet were all white like Lola, but then she had a perfect line where her fur was a mix of dark and light grey. It was pretty cool! I felt like their names fit well, because Pip seemed like a bit of a tomboy, whereas Lola was quite pretty and girly.

When I brought them home, I put them in their new enclosure. It didn't take long for little Pip to be exploring, but poor Lola hid for twenty-four hours until she came out to look around. It was the day before my eighteenth, and during my birthday party I was ridiculously protective of my new babies. My friends were trying to have fun and I'd tell them off for being too loud in case it scared them!

Around this period of time, I was still struggling quite a lot with my mental health. My tics weren't too bad, but my depression and other illnesses were really kicking my butt. Lola and Pip were amazing therapy for me and could calm me down within minutes. At home if I had panic attacks or was feeling low and weepy, I'd get one of the bunnies out and bring them inside for a cuddle.

I remember one evening I was so emotional I couldn't

stop crying, so I got Lola out for some time with her, and the poor little thing got soggy from my tears! They all rolled off my cheek and dripped on to her white fur as I cradled her.

My favourite thing to do with them was to sit with them in the rabbit run. They climbed all over me and sometimes Pip got a little sassy. She would tug at my shoelaces and dig at my jumper. One day when my friend Peter was round, he sat in with them and she nibbled his belt. He wasn't impressed.

They had a toy in their enclosure which had a bell inside. Sometimes in the middle of the night, I could hear the bell tinkling. It made me smile from ear to ear as I lay in my bed picturing them playing.

However, my absolute favourite memory of them happened one evening when I was really poorly with my mental health. It's such a precious memory and I just had to include it in my book. I had been crying, so Mum suggested I bring a bunny in. Lola let me pick her up, so I carried her carefully through to the living room and sat down with Mum.

As the three of us sat there, Beano wandered into the room and he perked up when he saw us. He jumped up on to the sofa with us. I was worried because he had never been so close to the rabbits before, and Beano was, as I've said, a great hunter! I became protective of Lola in case anything happened. But Beano was purring loudly. He was rubbing his head on us trying to get a fuss. My breathing calmed down and I couldn't help but smile. Beano came and squashed on to my knee with Lola. I felt so peaceful.

Beano began rubbing his head on Lola and gently nudging her with his little pink nose. It was such a sweet moment – my mum took her phone out and began recording. I watch this video often; it brings me great comfort. You can hear me sniffling in the background, but when this moment happened, the crying stopped. After rubbing himself on Lola and nuzzling into her soft white fur, Beano looks at the camera with his kind green eyes. That moment was so special.

# Meltdowns and Magical Moments

Okay, let's dive back into my school days.

As you'll remember, at this point I was struggling more than I ever had before. One afternoon, I was meant to be in maths class when I finally got to a breaking point. The teacher noticed I wasn't there but had been marked as in school for the rest of the day. They must have contacted my head of year because they knew I was vulnerable and struggling a lot. They went on a search looking for me.

I was actually hiding in the library, sitting at a table with my head in my hands. I knew I was supposed to be in a lesson, but at this time my depression was the worst it'd ever been, my thoughts were horrendous and there's no way I could have kept myself together in maths class.

I don't know how long it took them to find me; all I know is I raised my head from my hands to find my head of year in front of me, frantic and a bit out of breath.

'Evie? What are you doing in here?'

I didn't even know what to say. I couldn't explain it either.

'You're meant to be in maths right now. Is everything okay, Evie? We were worried about you.'

I felt so bad. I didn't mean to worry anyone; I was just so wrapped up in my own head, it didn't even feel like I was at school. I might as well have been anywhere.

'I'm so sorry ...' I managed to get out, my breathing uneven. I noticed his expression change, and he sat down opposite me.

'What's going on? You can tell me.' He smiled kindly, and I struggled to keep the tears in.

My chin started to wobble and before I fully knew what was happening, I was telling him about the horrible thoughts I was having. I don't want to go into what they were specifically, but they were awful. After it all came spilling out, he excused himself for a moment, and then told me that my mum was on her way. He sat with me for a bit to make sure I was safe and then I was ushered to his office.

When we got there, my mum was already sitting in a chair. I was shocked and thought she must have teleported or something?!

```
The teachers were very concerned for
Evie. She had disappeared from class
and hidden in the library. She was
distraught and saying things that were
concerning. We knew that day that things
needed to change drastically.
```

In the office, my head of year suggested something I really needed to hear.

'Don't come in next week, Evie. Please, take a break and come back when you feel more safe.'

Just like that, a crushing weight was lifted!

At first we weren't sure how a week off would work because I couldn't be left at home on my own. At this point, Mum was a teaching assistant, an amazing one too. My dad was also working full-time. Luckily the head teacher at Mum's school agreed that I could come in with Mum and help with small classroom jobs like setting up play areas, putting out supplies, etc. Mum worked at my old primary school, so it was going to be strange going back there again. But she thought it might be good for me to meet the kids and hopefully find my smile again. I was nervous at first because I felt so fragile, but Mum told me the kids were amazing and would love meeting me.

This was close to Christmas in 2015, so all the kids were excited for Santa to arrive. My mum worked with reception and the year 1 class – so from age four to six. I followed her around all day because I was too anxious to be on my own, but I think she was fine with that! Mum has always been so protective, but not in an overbearing way, just in a great parenting way. She makes me feel so safe.

On my first day, we walked into the assembly hall (this one is a lot less scary – especially when it's got four-year-old children running around in it!) and I saw loads of little ones dressed up in non-uniform for a Christmas party. One little girl caught my eye, dancing and spinning and loving the music. Her name was Naomi, and she was only four, but straight away I noticed how stunning she was. Her hair was beautiful. She had a head full of bouncy curls, big green eyes and the cutest smile. She was so full of life and joy, I couldn't help but smile with her. She attached herself to me pretty quickly and we held hands and danced together.

I found it difficult to understand her when she spoke,

then my mum told me she needed extra support. She was honestly the most adorable child I had ever seen.

Straight away my mood was boosted; I wasn't even thinking about those awful thoughts, they just disappeared whenever I was with her. I believe we were meant to meet that day. It's like all that I went through at school was worth it because it gave me the chance to meet her. So in a way I was grateful.

During our week together, I learnt more about Naomi. The more time we spent together, the more I started to under-stand the way she spoke. She was so smiley and had the most infectious laugh that just brightened up the room – you could hear it from down the corridor.

I came to know her mum, Jessica, too from seeing her at home time. Naomi (or 'Omi' as she called herself) really was a blessing in disguise; she couldn't have come along at a better time for me. When I was with her it didn't even feel like I had depression.

Usually, children ate in the hall with all their classmates and no teachers. However, Naomi, bless her, took ages to eat her dinner. She wanted to chat about her home life and her morning, and the bustle of the lunch hall distracted her. She ate her peas with her tiny fingers one by one, and it took her so long that it was time for lessons to begin again. So Mum suggested that I sit with Naomi while she ate her dinner, to chat with her, put her at ease and jog her along. I actually preferred this to sitting in the staffroom with the other teachers. They were all so lovely but my anxiety made me afraid that they didn't want me in school, and that they were all judging me.

I absolutely loved sitting with her. She was full of made-up stories about pretend families and she proudly told me about her lovely dog Betsy every day without fail. Even though it was so difficult to understand her, I could have listened to her chatting all day.

The week came to an end and, over the following days, I thought a lot about my time at the primary school. It made me smile thinking about all the lovely kids I met, and the memories of spending time with Naomi.

While I had been there, it got me thinking. All my life I had loved being around children; I thought I'd like to do a job with them, maybe a teaching assistant like Mum. People told me I was great with kids, especially in the later years as I gained more confidence.

After that week back at primary school, the thought of going back to my own school lingered in the back of my mind all weekend. Whenever I thought about being back in that environment, my heart sped up and I felt so panicky.

As much as I was dreading it, I braved it and went back. It was lovely to see Eve and my friends again. But, of course, just because I took a week off, it didn't mean I was 'cured' or that I wasn't depressed or anxious anymore. As soon as I was in the building all those feelings came flooding back; in fact, they were maybe even worse than before.

This was when I reached a second breaking point. I came home from school one day and had a meltdown. I was sobbing, not just crying, but inconsolable sobbing. My mum sat with me and I said, 'I can't go to school anymore, I can't.' For my parents it must have been really upsetting to see me like this. It just got too much for me; I was constantly scared when I was there, and it wasn't the teachers' fault or anything like that, I just felt that way.

Eve found it difficult because she didn't know how to help

me. She had never seen me like this. For years we had giggled together for hours, done really embarrassing best friend things, and were always laughing so much our jaws hurt from grinning. But now I rarely smiled, I didn't talk as much, I felt like I had shrunk so small. I had tried to continue at school but I couldn't keep going any longer.

It was hard for my brothers, too.

After that evening, me and my parents had a meeting with my head of year. They all decided the best thing for me was to leave school. In future I would be home-schooled. I was obviously quite pleased with this idea, and I couldn't wait to get out of there!

There were a few obstacles we had to overcome first to make it possible. Both my parents worked full-time. Yes, my mum worked in a school, but she couldn't be MY teacher because she was so busy. And I couldn't be home-schooled at my house, because no one was home during the day. So then Mum had an idea. We would get tutors for me, and I would be tutored at the primary school! The head teacher was lovely about this; she allowed me to be in school again, and allowed my tutors to be in the school too.

This was a good plan, because it meant that I could be with Mum and she could keep an eye on me during these difficult times, and it also meant . . . I could see Naomi again! Of course I wouldn't be in the classroom with the kids as often as I was during that week off school because I would be busy doing work with my tutors, but whenever I had finished I always spent my free time in the classroom with the children and with Naomi.

I was over the moon to see her again; we had such a special bond and she was excited to see me too. The feeling of having a child excited to see you, running towards you with a big smile on their face, really makes you feel so important. I finally felt like I had that little sister I'd always longed for. And it wasn't just Naomi; I had gotten to know the other children in her class and they all had great personalities.

Of course, my mental health issues hadn't disappeared just because I was no longer at secondary school. That place made my problems worse, but it wasn't the cause of them. Some days I had no motivation to do the work with my tutors, I was daydreamy and probably a bit difficult to teach sometimes. Some days I cried, and I felt so bad about it, like the staff were all thinking, 'Why is she here?' or, 'I wish she would leave.' These thoughts upset me greatly, but they were hard to ignore. All the staff were so lovely to me, and no one actually made me feel this way; it was just my pesky anxiety telling me things that aren't true.

My anxiety made me do some things which now seem really bizarre. At lunchtime I sometimes stayed in the library, but other times I would sit in the staffroom with all the teachers and Mum. I remember one lunchtime I had finished eating an apple, and I wanted to get up and put it in the bin which was literally only a few feet across the room, but I was too anxious to be the only one standing up, and I didn't want anyone staring at me, so I sat there with the apple core turning brown in my hands.

At that time I was fifteen, and my anxiety was a lot worse than what it is now. It might seem so odd to some of you reading that, but mental health can have strange effects on us. For you readers with anxiety or social anxiety, I'm sure you may find it relatable in some way.

Home-schooling had its pros – I was out of my old comprehensive school and could start healing from my time there, and a big bonus was obviously seeing Naomi's lovely face again – but it also had its cons, which I had never thought about until I went through it myself.

It's lonely. I wasn't with Eve every day anymore and that was the first time since we were five. It was a big change for the both of us.

My thoughts told me that my friends were glad I was gone because they didn't have to be around my miserable self any longer and they didn't miss me. Which was a load of rubbish.

I found myself feeling really disconnected from everyone – it wasn't a nice feeling at all. I almost felt jealous of my friends, that they were continuing their time at school, and were doing okay, and I wasn't.

I also missed out on prom. Technically I chose not to go, but to this day I wish I had. I have to remember that at the time I was too poorly and I wouldn't have been able to enjoy it. Seeing photos of my friends in their beautiful dresses made me sad that I wasn't in those pictures with them, where I should have been. Me and Eve going to prom together after being best friends for years and years would have been a really special moment. You looked stunning, Eve

My tutors helped me to study for my upcoming GCSE exams, but first I had to get over my fear of school because that's where I would have to sit them. It used to be that even being outside the building made me panic, so I had a long way to go. My maths tutor had an idea. She would drive me from the primary school and up to my old secondary school that I was terrified of. In the beginning, when we found a spot in the car park, I didn't want to get out of the car. So that's what we did, we just sat in her small car for five or ten minutes, watching people go in and out of the school.

Even sitting outside, my anxiety was creeping up on me.

After that period of time, we drove back to the primary school. When that started getting easier, we could begin building it up more, so, for example, we would go and sit on a bench outside the school.

Eventually, we took it up another level. I had to get used to being in the building again, so my tutor and I would sit in the library of my secondary school, and she would tutor me there. Not for the whole time, just half an hour or so. I hated it. I couldn't concentrate at all. The fear of being inside the school just made me freeze up. Some of the other students in my year didn't make it easy, either, but I'm not going to go into that.

For the real GCSE exams, I was allowed to sit in a separate room, so I wouldn't be in the giant hall with everyone else. This would have caused me far too much stress and I would never have been able to actually write anything down. I was also allowed some extra time.

During the exams, I managed to get my head down and I did answer most questions if not all of them. My Tourette's was mild at this point so I didn't have to worry about shouting or throwing anything!

I didn't do great in my exams, but I did okay considering how unwell I was and what I'd been through. I got a B in R.E. (Religious Education) which really shocked me given that I got an F in the mock exam!!

I saw lots of posts on Facebook of people sharing how well they had done and posting pictures of their As and A*s. I couldn't help but compare myself to them. I had failed roughly five exams and only passed about two! Of course, I failed maths. Which I totally expected. I just don't get numbers! It all looks so alien to me.

After the exams, our time at secondary school came to an

end. I was already worrying about being separated from all my friends, but I know now it's just a part of life.

It makes me sad that on leavers' day, while everyone was getting their T-shirts signed, hugging people, saying goodbye and getting a yearbook, I was in a small back room having a maths lesson, which I had to do since I didn't pass in my GCSEs. I felt so left out. It was a rubbish feeling. I would have liked to see some of my teachers again; I didn't get to say bye to them properly like everyone else did.

When the lesson eventually finished my tutor let me go and see some of my friends. They all had signatures covering their shirts, some had red faces from crying. They got me a yearbook and some people signed it for me which was nice.

I was also of course leaving the primary school where I had been home-schooled, and this was upsetting because I thought that would be the end of my time with Naomi. However, Naomi's lovely mum Jessica told me I could keep seeing her outside of school. I cannot put into words how happy this made me.

I remember when I saw her outside of school for the first time. I visited their house and I couldn't contain myself, I was so excited. We jumped around on the bouncy castle in their garden, and I met Naomi's little sister Yasmin for the first time. A beautiful little toddler with brown eyes and brown curls, she was so shy the day I met her. She was only two at the time, and still had some of her baby chub! She looked adorable in her pink shorts and a tiny T-shirt, and with her baby curls bouncy on her head.

Yasmin has always been so sweet and caring – she's a bit crackers now but she's gorgeous! When she was a little younger, if we were playing a game and I pretended to be hurt or dead, Yasmin really thought I was injured and came to check if I was okay with this worried look on her face. Whereas Naomi thought it was hilarious!

Naomi was so excited to see me outside of the school environment and was desperate to show me everything in her house. Especially her beloved dog Betsy. She is a bundle of energy, and pees all over you when she's happy to see you! Betsy, I mean, not Naomi . . .

Naomi looked beautiful and she knew it. That first day I went to her house, she bounced around and fell down in a heap and said, 'Take my picture!' She had just fallen down but she looked like a model. All her curls were spread out and perfectly placed.

We all took pictures together and I was so happy to finally have photos with my two surrogate sisters. Now I could show them to my friends and tell them all about these girls who were everything to me.

Naomi and Yasmin were my lifeline. I was in such a dark place when I met them, wanting to give up, but they turned it all around. Their smiles and infectious laughs made me feel so warm. The love they had for me reminded me that I was enough.

After this day we continued to see each other regularly; we had sleepovers and days out, and when I was asked what I wanted to do for my birthday, every year I would say I wanted to see my girls, and I still say that now!

It's been five years now since that day on the bouncy castle, and Naomi and Yasmin are growing up. Naomi is ten as I write this, and Yasmin is seven. It's been five amazing years with them, so many memories and giggles.

Due to Covid we haven't seen each other as much as we usually would. It's been over a year since our last sleepover and my heart aches, I miss them so much.

One sleepover, it was only Naomi because Yasmin was too little at the time, and Naomi and I slept in my room. I read her a bedtime story and we squished into my single bed for a cuddle before settling down. It took me ages to get Naomi to feel sleepy because she wanted to chat about every thought that popped into her head. Eventually she nodded off, so I slithered out of my bed and into a roll-up bed we put on the floor.

The next morning I woke up before her. I waited a while until I noticed the time, then I gently sat down next to her where she was still fast asleep. I gave her a kiss and a cuddle and said her name quietly. Her eyes opened, looking around as if she wasn't sure where she was. She realised I was right in front of her and said 'Evie!' and snuggled into me.

I felt so loved in that moment. She had forgotten that she was at my house for a sleepover so she wasn't expecting to wake up there, but her reaction to me being the first thing she saw when she woke up was just so heart-warming.

When the time was right, I told my girls about my Tourette's. As they grew older and became more mature, they began asking questions. Yasmin asked her mum Jessica why I said 'beans' all the time!

We were having lunch together in my dining room, when my Nonidentical Twin flung yoghurt all over Naomi. We all giggled around helplessly and I decided then would be a perfect time to explain. I told them my brain was a little different, and said it's called 'Tourette's' and they were both fascinated. On the way home Naomi asked so many questions, it was lovely. And just as I thought they would, they fully accepted me and didn't see me any differently.

They have seen me in my wheelchair and using my walker, but they don't mind at all. Yasmin, being the sweetie she is, likes to glance at me every now and then to check I'm all right.

It has been incredible to watch my girls grow up. I will forever be grateful to have been part of their lives. I'm so proud of Naomi and Yasmin and slightly jealous of how beautiful they both are!

Their mum Jessica wanted to add this:

> The girls love you, Evie, you're their family. You and your family have always been there for us no matter what you have been going through. You are an inspiration, not only to us but so many people.
>
> I will always remember picking Naomi up from school and your mum coming out and introducing herself and wanting to talk about Naomi. I remember thinking she's only been here five minutes, what has she done now!
>
> But she explained that yourself and Naomi had hit it off and you wanted to keep seeing each other. We exchanged numbers, became Facebook friends and the rest is history. You saved Naomi too, that's why you will always be together. I was so worried about her starting school but knowing you were there for her made it so much easier, and I can never repay you for that.

# A New Chapter

Since I had now left school, I had to figure out what I wanted to study at college. I told Mum I would love to work with animals, and after a bit of searching, she helped me find a college with an animal care course. I saw pictures of students with the animals and I couldn't believe it, it seemed almost too good to be true. I was nervous to be in a school environment again, when I had got used to home-schooling and private tutoring, so I knew it was going to be difficult, but I wanted to try.

Mum and I spoke to the college about my issues, and how anxious and unwell I had been. I was put into a special unit, for people with disabilities and those who needed extra help. So I wasn't actually going to be in the mainstream section of the college, but we would walk up to the animal care building.

I was okay with this idea, but it felt strange. I was a teenager: I wanted to be like everyone else.

I had a starter day, where I went to the unit for an afternoon to meet the staff, look around and see the animals. The staff were lovely, and the variety of animals was truly amazing. They had a small animal section with everything from rabbits, guinea pigs, hamsters, mice and gerbils to chinchillas and even a couple of chipmunks. They had dog kennels with all different breeds in, and then a farm, with cows, sheep, pigs – it was so cool!

And there was a reptile room, with geckos and lizards – one was ginormous! Plus snakes of all different sizes, and they had a place where they kept the live bugs to feed them. Yuck! They even had an aquatic room, with all kinds of fish. I loved watching them. It was so relaxing.

I was very quiet during this visit, I just felt so nervous being in a new environment, but I assumed that, like most people, once I was more comfortable there I would be fine speaking to others and using my voice.

I came away from this day looking forward to starting there. I was more excited about the animals than the people!

Something else happened around this time, though, that did introduce me to new faces I would look forward to seeing time and again. Through my early teen years, social media was never a big thing for me. I liked chatting to friends and watching videos online, but I didn't particularly participate in posting online much. I posted the odd photo of my pets, a selfie here and there.

Then, around the time I was starting college, I discovered an app called Musical.ly (now known as TikTok!). I love music and when I saw the app it looked like a nice safe space and a great way to express yourself. I didn't want to just post lip-syncing videos like everyone else, so I decided to use it as a place to practise sign language, and sign along to songs. I'd decided to start learning sign language when I realised not enough people have any knowledge of this language. If I were to come across a deaf person, I wanted to know I'd be able to communicate with them. Expressing myself just using my hands felt beautiful, and I did it in a way where I was being as respectful to the deaf community as I could be.

One of the reasons I liked using this platform was because not many of my friends or people from my school followed me on it, so I could post without fear of judgement. I also found a whole new community I didn't really know existed: the signing community. Through it I met a varied group of people – some hard of hearing, some deaf, some hearing – and it was amazing to be a part of that.

My account was fairly small, but soon I had over 10,000 followers, which now seems like barely anything! Yet at the time it was exciting. People liked my boho style and my sign language, and it was lovely to have people lifting me up and encouraging me. It felt incredible having this whole world separate from my day-to-day life in college.

I don't remember a lot from my first proper day at college, but I will tell you what I do recall.

I was so anxious. This really was a new chapter in my life, and I didn't have Eve with me anymore, so I was worried I was going to be lonely. While I noticed very quickly that there were quite a few other neurodivergent people in my unit, none of them had the same issues as me, so I still felt a bit like the odd one out.

As soon as I was in college I didn't speak. At first, I just thought this was a result of my social anxiety and that once I had settled in I would come out of my shell a bit, so I wasn't too worried. Whenever the staff spoke to me I just nodded or shook my head. I still smiled so at least I didn't look totally odd!

As well as classes with the animals, we had other lessons too – I still had to do maths! When we did get to go to the animal care building, we started off cleaning out the animals and feeding them.

Some of you might find this weird, but my favourite animals to work with in the small animal section were the mice. Some people don't like them because they say they are too similar to rats, but I think they're so cute. I loved their little pink feet, their noses and whiskers. There was one little white mouse who was the runt of the litter. It was actually more of an off-white colour, and I noticed a sign on the glass saying that it was poorly. I took it out to have a look at it, and the poor little thing was so scruffy. It had bald spots and very red skin. It wasn't a baby but it was teeny-tiny. All the animals at the college had great enclosures and were very well cared for, but this mouse was unfortunately just a bit unwell – sometimes that's the way things go.

As you know I am a huge rabbit lover. I think they're actually quite misunderstood. Some people get them as pets and put them in small hutches and don't interact with them much because they think they just sit there and do nothing, a bit like having a pet fish or something. Rabbits are actually very sociable and loving; you can teach them tricks and, if they are really happy, they can have zoomies! So I liked being with the rabbits too. The college had quite a few, at least seven or eight. One of them was a rex rabbit called Charlotte. If you aren't familiar with the breed, rex rabbits are mostly well-known for their fur texture, which is ridiculously soft – so soft it's almost like you aren't touching anything at all. All the rabbits there were difficult to catch and tricky to pick up, but when I could, it was really soothing.

I feel that being in the separate unit because of my issues held me back, and I didn't get to be with the animals as much as the students in the mainstream section. But on a few occasions we did go up to the farm. I remember one day going up there and there were around seven or eight calves. They were so cute; they had such pretty eyes and eyelashes. One of them started suckling on my finger! We had to wear PPE-like overalls, and even the smallest size was far too big for me. I'm quite petite so I looked a bit silly in such baggy big blue overalls.

We also went to see the pigs, and started mucking them out. I didn't mind this; I'm used to cleaning out rabbit poop at home and, although it's not quite the same, the smell and look of pig poo didn't faze me much. The pigs all wandered around us and they started to get cheeky. I was holding a big heavy shovel, and one pig trotted over to me and began biting my wellies. I was laughing and trying to shake him off, but then this naughty pig started trying to take the shovel out of my hand! It was putting its wet snout and mouth round the shovel and roughly tugging on it. This cheeky chap was surprisingly strong. I was worried I was going to lose a fight to a pig! It was moments like this that made all the struggles at college worthwhile.

# Losing My Voice

The first few months of college went by and I hadn't made any proper friends yet. To be fair, I probably didn't help myself much because I didn't speak to anyone! My silence, which I had initially thought was a temporary result of my anxiety, hadn't let up at all. When I say that, I mean I didn't speak a single word all day – I never used my voice box at all until I got through my front door at home.

As the months passed at my new college, I still wasn't speaking. I eventually realised that me being silent wasn't just because I was a little shy. I actually had no choice in it. I couldn't say a word even if I really wanted to. For example (this is just an extreme illustration to get my point across), even if I'd had a large open wound, I wouldn't have been able to speak and tell anyone, I would have just pointed or shown them. It really wasn't good.

During our lessons, everyone in the class (our classes were fairly small since we were in a unit) was given an individual goal for that lesson which suited them. Everyone's aim was different, and the staff and support teachers began making my goal to say one word or a few words that lesson.

At this time, I never achieved these goals. This continued for months and months.

I was in my first year at this college when I suffered another big gymnastics injury – I dislocated my elbow. It was more damage to my left elbow, which I severely broke in 2011, so I think maybe the bone had some weakness in it from then. It happened when I was practising for the Christmas displays. What's annoying in hindsight is that I should have already left for the day, but my partner Jenny and I decided to stay for another hour to get more practice in. If only I had gone home when I was meant to!

I knew straight away what had happened because it felt just like last time. It was only when I clutched my elbow that I realised something had occurred that didn't happen in 2011. My elbow had caved in. This made me feel very queasy!

My coach and my dad helped me off the gym floor, where I dramatically fainted before being taken to hospital. All of this meant that I was in a pink cast with a collar and cuff, so obviously at college I was going to struggle with writing, carrying things around, and getting changed into the PPE to work with the animals. Getting help with these things is nearly impossible when you're unable to speak, and I found myself getting even more frustrated.

Luckily, my lovely teacher bought me a lined-paper note-book, so I could write down anything I needed help with. So instead of me sitting in silence when I needed something, I would write it down and show it to someone. I really appreciated this gesture, it just made me feel accepted, and the staff never got angry with me for not speaking. They knew I was perfectly chatty at home, so it must have been frustrating for them not being able to get a word out of me, but they were all so kind.

My maths teacher would sometimes make a joke about me maybe speaking to her that lesson, and of course I usually didn't and she was never cross with me; she just said we could try again next time.

I know that I wasn't the easiest to be around. Although they were used to people with disabilities because of the unit I was in, the vast majority of the other students were very talkative.

I do feel guilty because some of them would try to start a conversation with me and say, 'Hi Evie', but I would just smile. I hated looking rude but I really could not get any words out. I liked it when teachers asked me a yes or no question because I could just nod or shake my head, but when they asked a question like, 'What did you do at the weekend?' I knew what they were trying to do – they were trying to encourage me to reply. It was these situations, where I couldn't nod or shake my head as an answer, that made me anxious. My whole body felt like it was shrinking and my heart would start pounding. I knew I must have looked silly, but all I could do was shrug my shoulders. I knew exactly what I did at the weekend, maybe I did something exciting and I wanted to tell them all about it, but I couldn't so I just shrugged.

I remember hearing the words 'selective mutism' for the first time. It was very early days at college. I was sat at a computer desk and the teachers were introducing themselves and trying to ask me for my name. I couldn't answer them.

I then heard a teacher mutter to another member of staff behind me, and all I could make out was those two words. I didn't mind, I just didn't know anything at all about selective mutism so I was intrigued. A therapist later told me this was most likely what I was experiencing. It wasn't exactly a shock to me because I knew I wasn't simply shy in college. But it was weird for my friends and family because, for them, I was totally down-to-earth and talkative.

'I can't imagine you being silent!' Eve said to me when I talked to her about how frustrating it was. All those years she has known me, we have never stopped chatting and messing about. So for her to imagine me being so silent and reserved was strange for her.

If you know someone with selective mutism, or perhaps you are a teacher and one of your students is a selective mute, the kindest thing you can do is be patient. Selective mutism is a complex anxiety disorder, which usually appears in children, but for some, like me, it can start in their early/middle teen years. People may look at a child with selective mutism and think they are rude or disobedient, when in fact they aren't choosing to be silent – they literally can't speak. Our bodies will not let us.

Don't leave us out just because we might not respond; we still like to feel included, just accept that we won't be very chatty. An individual with SM requires a lot of patience to allow them to speak in their own time, and the truth is that if the person feels as if they are being rushed, it will most likely make their mutism worse and it will take longer for them to be able to speak.

However, in some cases, the individual may never speak in a certain environment, or they might make some progress and speak to only one or two people. For example, even after being at that college for two and a half years, a lot of the students in the unit I was in have never heard my voice.

Being mute is quite lonely; my mental health was still pretty poor, and I was still depressed. It was also at this time that I began having more tics than those hiccup sounds.

The first one I noticed was my elbow and head jerking at the same time. I sometimes noticed that my legs would randomly jump, but I thought these were anxiety twitches. When I think right back to just before my first day at college (this would have been 2016) I was bashing my knuckles together and I couldn't stop, even when the pain was so bad. Afterwards my hands were black and blue and swollen.

Eventually, after almost a year, I began speaking a few words to a very, very small number of people I felt most comfortable with. My speech was still very limited but even so it was a step forward!

It's so important for us to recognise and celebrate our achievements, no matter how small or silly they may seem. Me beginning to say a few words was huge, and I was so proud of myself, and the teachers didn't make a big fuss about it because that would have been a little intimidating, but I could see they were really happy with me and my progress.

Remember that, whatever you are going through, whatever obstacles life has thrown at you, you can get past them and it will get better. It may sound a bit clichéd, and I used to feel a little irritated when someone said that to me! But I honestly promise you that things can get brighter.

It's great for me to dwell on these positives, because it was around this time in 2016 that the third episode that completely changed my life for ever took place.

# A Shocking Development

I took taxis to college each morning because I was too anxious to take the bus by myself. I had tried to work through it with counsellors but I just couldn't do it. It made my heart race and I felt so unsafe.

When I got there, I had to wait outside the building with everyone else until the teachers were ready to let us in – as they sometimes had meetings first thing. One day, during a period when my mental health and depression were beginning to slip again, we were waiting to go in when my shoulders began shrugging and twitching uncontrollably. I was in a very dissociative state and wasn't really aware of what I was doing. I really don't remember much after this – there are lots of gaps.

Next thing I knew, I was sitting on a bean bag in the common room with other students walking around just getting on with their day. I had no idea how I'd got there. I felt so odd, like I wasn't even me. My head space was just blank and clueless; I had no idea what was going on and I didn't even feel like I really knew where I was. Not too long later, I went into a seizure. I still remember the start of it – my body was twitching uncontrollably. I was only aware for maybe a couple of minutes; after that, I fell unconscious. I wish I could give you more details but I just don't know what was going on around me during the seizure. I imagine the staff were panicking since I had never had one before in my life.

It's a general rule that whenever anyone has a seizure for the first time, you have to phone emergency services. So an ambulance was called; they put a cannula into my arm and stopped the seizure with a drug called diazepam. Time then jumped to me lying in the ambulance. Even now, I still don't remember what happened to me during my first ever seizure. I had no clue how much of an impact these episodes would have on me from then on.

After that day at college, the seizures continued and have never stopped since. I didn't understand why they were happening; I knew my mental health was pretty appalling so I did think it was maybe linked to that. I remember telling Eve about them and her asking 'Do you know why you have them?' She was looking at me so concerned. I didn't have any explanation to give her. She was of course brilliant about that and comforted me – it was so good to have her support, because it was so terrifying to have my body behave in a certain way and doctors not have an explanation as to why.

As the years passed, I started having seizures more regularly. However, I always try to look for the positives, and I was so excited to find out in 2018 that I would no longer be in the separate unit; I would be in the mainstream college.

I still needed support, but it felt like a huge step in the right direction. We took this decision because I was making great progress with my speech, saying sentences to a handful of people, and I was dealing with being at college better than I had been. In that unit I was being held back from working with animals properly.

I also made some new friends around this time, which gave me even more to look forward to outside of college. One of them was a lovely person called Peter. He was actually a friend of a friend, who was at university. My initial impression of him was that he seemed really funny. However, the first day we met we didn't speak a word to each other!

Over time we began messaging a lot online and eventually started hanging out together. Within a few months we were best friends. We hung out more and more, spending some really lovely days together. My favourite thing to do with him was picnicking by the river, or taking lovely walks through nature.

Although it was amazing to have someone like that in my life, my health didn't give me a break. In February 2018, I was sitting on the couch watching TV and I felt a seizure coming on. I'm used to this feeling now, but it's still not nice at all. I usually get a headache, above one eye or both, and I begin feeling really far away, like I'm not really here. I also start to struggle to understand sentences when people are speaking to me. I can hear them, but I can't process the words. My parents say that my face completely changes and I go very vacant.

Eventually I had a seizure, a full-body convulsion seizure but it was no different to my usual ones – I think it lasted around ten minutes. I began coming out of it – you can usually tell because the convulsions slow down before stopping completely, and then the eyes begin to focus again instead of just blankly staring.

Mum was sitting next to me. 'You okay, sweetheart? You back with us?'

Something wasn't right. 'I think so,' I said. Then: 'Wait . . . I can't move my legs, Mum.' My heart started to speed up and I began getting upset.

'What? Not at all?'

She started squeezing my legs and my toes to see if I could feel it, which I could. I could feel her touching them, I just couldn't lift them or even wiggle my toes. They were just dead weight. This felt odd because I felt like I could move them if I really tried but they wouldn't budge. I just couldn't get my brain to connect with my legs. Then when I tried bearing weight and walking, my ankles twisted inwards and my body just slumped.

That evening my parents took me to hospital. We had to get a wheelchair so I could actually get inside the hospital. I remember being helped out of the car as my legs just dangled there.

The doctors were baffled, and said that all my tests were normal. To be honest, they didn't do many. I had my blood drawn, they tested my reflexes and that was about it. I was upset about this because I thought perhaps a problem would have shown up on an MRI or something. I sat in the hospital room with Mum and just cried. I didn't understand why my legs didn't work when there was apparently nothing wrong with me.

The doctor I saw was lovely; he asked me to try to take a few steps. I clung to his arm; he was really supportive and encouraging but I couldn't help feeling a bit embarrassed because my legs looked so weird and my feet were in funny positions. I sat back down and the doctor apologised for not knowing what was wrong.

Eventually they sent me home, still paralysed from the waist down. There wasn't anything they could do. I was told to rest and see if I recovered. I was hoping maybe I would wake up after a good sleep and my legs would be as they were. But I was wrong. My legs took almost a month to get back to normal again. I often had a tingly feeling in my legs, and sometimes they felt super-painful.

I was unable to do anything myself; even if I wanted the TV on, someone had to do it for me. I struggled to change myself, get in and out of the shower, get myself to the table for dinner, all those small things we take for granted were taken away. During all this, I coped using humour and just smiling through it. I made jokes about how weird my legs looked, and had a good giggle with my parents as they tried to move me around the house, crashing into walls and stumbling about!

It was 2018 when I got my first mobility aid. We borrowed some crutches from a neighbour, but my legs were paralysed so this wasn't quite enough to help me get around. We then bought a wheelchair.

Getting used to being in public in a wheelchair was strange. I almost felt like I shouldn't be in a wheelchair, if that makes sense? As if my problem wasn't severe enough, although I literally couldn't walk.

I have been in and out of a wheelchair for three years so far and I'm not embarrassed anymore. If I need a little help to get around then that's what I need, there's no shame in that. Without my wheelchair, there would be times when I'd just be stuck in the house and have no independence. So, if I was having a flare-up, at least with my wheels I could still go out for a stroll with my family.

Recovery from my first experience of paralysis came eventually, although weirdly my legs didn't recover at the same time. My left leg came back quicker than my right leg, so there was a time when I could lift my left leg and move it around okay, but my right leg was still paralysed, which was bizarre. It was so frustrating!

Then, after getting full mobility back, the same thing happened five months later. So I was back in a wheelchair again. Thankfully, the paralysis didn't last as long that time, and my legs were normal again after a week or so.

My Grandma Isabel and Granddad Bill, bless them, were, like the rest of us, so worried. They were just as much in the dark as I was. They rang us regularly asking for updates, and even sent me a stuffed dog, with wild fluffy ears and huge eyes. Having my family rally around me made me feel so much better.

And then . . . as if I hadn't had enough bad luck with my health, two months after that, I had a seizure and when I came out of it my right arm was paralysed. It was completely floppy. I tried to continue with normal things, but even going to the toilet was extremely difficult. I was at college at that time too, and going there with a paralysed arm dangling down by my side was slightly weird.

A few months earlier, I had met my best friend at college, a sweet girl called Chloe, who's deaf. The first time Chloe and I met I was in a wheelchair with paralysed legs. The teachers said we would be good together because I knew sign language, but I was too nervous to talk to her for ages, even though she was so smiley. It literally took me weeks to approach her, because, yes, I knew sign language, but I had never actually used it to speak to a deaf person before. I remember anxiously walking up to her and signing, 'I like your hair' because she has lovely thick brown wavy hair. She said thank you and we talked for a while. Eventually we were best friends, and tried to spend all day together. It was great because we could gossip about people and they wouldn't understand what we were saying!

But when my arm was paralysed, it made talking to each other really difficult. Luckily, we made it work and she could mostly understand me okay. To spell something out I used American Sign Language (ASL), since that alphabet is all on one hand. I remember us being in class together when I noticed my paralysed hand had turned blotchy and purple. I told my support teacher and they put my arm in a sling to keep it elevated so the circulation would be better. This was much more dignified than walking around with my arm flopping about like a fish! My family were such gems about it too. My brother Joshua would help me out a bit by doing things like tying my shoelaces for me.

Thankfully, four or five days later my hand was normal again. I remember the night I got some movement back. I tried doing sign language to some calm music – it was quite painful after being dead weight for a while, but I was so happy to be able to move it again!

For two years these sorts of things happened and I didn't have a clue what was causing them. Terrifying, don't you think? And then – finally – I received a diagnosis. The doctors said it was a neurological disorder called FND (functional neurological disorder). This is another complex condition which is widely misunderstood.

FND is an issue with the functioning of the nervous system, and the brain sending the wrong signals. The thing I hate most about FND is that your legs can be literally paralysed – like mine were – but all scans will be totally normal.

In some ways, news of this diagnosis was devastating. When something is wrong with you, you want an answer so you can look for a cure, but with FND there is none. It happens because, when our brains are overloaded and we are stressed or going through mental health issues, we sometimes get physical symptoms. Have you ever come home after a really long or stressful day with a banging headache? FND is basically a more extreme version of this.

The doctors said that because I was healing from trauma (the details of which I am afraid I am unable to share) and poor mental health at the time, my brain was basically saying, 'Nope! I can't handle this!' and reacting in debilitating ways.

However, sometimes, there is no cause or trigger for these symptoms. I often have bad FND days even when I am not the slightest bit stressed.

FND has many symptoms, but not everyone experiences all of the following:

- Muscle weakness
- Paralysis
- Muscle locking
- Pain throughout the body
- Headaches
- In some cases, temporary blindness or deafness
- Dizziness
- Bladder problems
- Speech issues (slurred or loss of speech)

- Memory loss
- Numbness and tingling sensations
- Seizures and tremors
- Brain fog

I had only ever had to deal with mental illnesses in my head, which did sometimes come out as physical symptoms, like the hair loss and migraines I explained earlier. However, this was a new extreme and nothing I ever thought would happen to me. Suddenly having a new condition was so difficult to get used to.

My seizures happened every day for a long time. This meant that wherever I went I was basically just waiting to have a seizure. Going into shops was a worry because I was so anxious I was going to have a seizure and cause a big fuss. I felt safe having them at home because my family are all so amazing and I know that no one judges me. I know I wasn't really being judged at college, but it was a lot scarier having a seizure there because I didn't know anyone that well. So for them to see me in that state, I felt so vulnerable.

I've had seizures in all kinds of places. Many different shops, a beach, on a boat, in the car, in the park, on the stairs, by a river – I've lost count. My favourite place (not that you can really have a favourite place to have a seizure!) was the beach, because although it was a little overwhelming to regain consciousness outside in the bright light, I could hear seagulls and the waves crashing.

It was frustrating not knowing when or where I'd have them – or who I'd be in front of at the time. The first time Peter came to my house, we were chilling in the living room, watching a movie, when, typically, I had a tonic-clonic seizure (more about these on page 112). It was so long and severe that an ambulance had to be called. Great first impression!

Peter was a little shaken up since he hadn't even seen me have a mild seizure, let alone a big one. After that night I was expecting to get a message saying he didn't want to hang out anymore. Which I know sounds ridiculous, but at the time I had no clue how people would react to my health problems.

Peter witnessed many more seizures. He got used to them, and is so amazing when I have one now. He holds me, tells me that I'm okay, reminding me of where I am and who I'm with. He even had to dive to catch me once. We were having a lovely day by the riverbank, and, as we were walking back, he said I just stopped walking and stared blankly. I started falling and he told me afterwards that he had to quickly scoop in and catch me. My knight in shining armour!

He really is one in a million. Not everyone feels comfortable witnessing a seizure, and I fully understand that. I've seen other people have a seizure and it's really scary.

Peter worries about me, of course, but he doesn't let it show, and if I sense a seizure coming on, I feel totally safe knowing he's with me. One seizure I had, he took his scarf off and placed it under my head, knowing it was going to get dirt and dribble on it. I felt so awful afterwards that his lovely scarf had all my saliva on it! But Peter just didn't mind at all.

When people hear the word 'seizure' they picture someone on the ground, thrashing about, foaming at the mouth and violently convulsing. Although some seizures are like this, there are actually many different types. I'm 'blessed' enough to have a lot of them(!).

The 'smallest' seizure is called an absent seizure, also

known as a petit mal seizure. This is where the person stares into space, unconscious for five to fifteen seconds. These seizures are easily missed, and can go unrecognised for a while because it just looks as if the person is day-dreaming. My parents can usually tell when I'm having an absence because my eyebrows go up and down, sort of as if I'm flirting!

During an absent seizure, the person is unable to hear you or respond, so you just have to wait till they have come out of it. I sometimes don't even realise I've had one, but if I'm watching TV I can easily tell because I notice I've missed a bit although I was watching the whole time. If I was in class at college, I could tell because people may have moved around, or they were talking about something else. My absent seizures actually started a while after the 'big' seizures, which is unusual. These ones don't bother me too much; they just make me feel a little drowsy. I've had a few absent seizures while writing this book, and I had to take a little break because I was finding it diffi-cult to focus.

The type of seizure that's sort of in the middle is a partial seizure. The way this seizure presents itself can be different depending on the person. They last longer than an absent seizure, but aren't full-body seizures. For me, I become extremely unresponsive and sometimes lose the use of my limbs. My jaw twitches and I might dribble a little bit. My head drops every now and then, and my arms twitch and jump. I also occasionally smack my lips or look as if I'm chewing something. These seizures actually can take longer to come out of. They feel so strange; I sometimes drift in and out of consciousness which I highly dislike. I'd rather be unconscious the whole time. I hate being conscious while my body is shaking, my face is still drooping and I have saliva running down my chin. As a very self-aware woman, it's not pretty!

Then, of course, we have the full-body seizures, also called grand mal seizures or tonic-clonics. These are my least favourite and are the ones that can send me to hospital. They are awful, though I'm not sure that word is strong enough. This was the very first seizure I ever had – what a way to kick things off!

Once in a while I have ones that aren't too bad. I convulse for five or ten minutes and come out of it with no aches or pains. The ones I used to have when they first started could last over an hour – which is crazy. It felt afterwards like I had just run at least two marathons with weights round my ankles.

These seizures are usually the most dangerous. They can make us fall down or collapse, which, if we are in the wrong place at the wrong time, can result in injuries. My grand mal seizures always start off with absent seizures and a headache. Whenever I feel those warning signs now, although it's been years, I still think, 'Oh God, here we go.'

My whole body convulses, I dribble, I may have difficulty breathing, my jaw can dislocate and all my muscles are so painful. I hate it when my jaw dislocates; if I come out of a seizure and my jaw has popped out, I know it was a bad one. I don't like people touching it so I just wriggle it around until it pops back in.

I have of course had my seizures investigated by an EEG (an electroencephalogram, if you want the whole name!). An EEG is when they attach lots of wires and electrodes to your head to monitor your brainwaves. They do things like make you hyperventilate, and flash a light at you, as this is a common trigger for seizures, especially in epilepsy.

My first EEG was done in one afternoon; I was really nervous as I didn't know what to expect. The results of this one were a little odd. They showed that during my test there had been some abnormal brain activity. However, they couldn't say whether this meant epilepsy or not.

So I had another EEG in 2019, but this time I stayed in hospital for four days. The day I had to arrive at hospital was actually on Joshua's birthday. So we all got up early for him to open presents before I left.

I felt awful that the timing was so unfortunate but Joshua of course understood that it couldn't be helped, and we had a big hug before I left.

This was the first time I have ever been in hospital by myself without my mum. However, she is never far away! She stayed in a hotel across the street and came every day during visiting hours. Talk about being a mummy's girl!

Eventually my results came back. My seizures were, as we suspected, not epileptic. During the two I had while in hospital, no brain abnormalities were detected. They did, however, tell me they found epileptiform activity in my sleep, meaning there were signs of seizure activity. I was told that if I drank too much alcohol or was extremely fatigued, I was susceptible to an epileptic seizure. I have been scared of this ever since!

Although it was great to know I didn't have epilepsy, not having a reason for them made me feel a little as if my seizures weren't valid. Non-epileptic seizures have a huge stigma around them, and are sometimes dismissed and overlooked. It shouldn't be this way. For a long time it made me ashamed to say my seizures weren't epileptic, because I was worried people would just shrug them off or not really believe me. I'm hoping to change the way non-epileptic seizures are viewed and treated.

Learning to accept myself with seizures has been a long, long journey. I didn't want to accept them. They're just horrible things that take away chunks of time and make me look ridiculous. I was mortified to have a seizure in front of anyone who wasn't close family or friends. Because, let's be honest, seizures aren't very attractive. With my mouth drooping to one side, slobber creeping down my face, it doesn't exactly paint a pretty picture.

Over time, I realised that my seizures weren't going anywhere. I started taking it all in my stride and making jokes about it. Now we often laugh about the way I look during a seizure, and it does help. Using humour as a coping mechanism isn't for everyone, and some people don't understand it, but I've spent years wasting my time feeling low about my seizures, and now being able to joke about it actually makes me more confident about them. I still don't like the way I look while seizing, but I can't help it; and, like my Tourette's, I can't control it, so there's really no point feeling so ashamed of it. And on the plus side, from years of practice, I am so good now at recognising when I'm going to have a seizure that I am able to get myself into a position where I am safe from harm.

Ideally, if you have a seizure or someone near you has one, there would be somebody else nearby or who you could call who has had experience caring for someone with a seizure, or some training on what to do. Especially if you're under 18, please don't try to look after someone who's having a bad seizure by yourself – you should get help. But in case it's helpful, below are some top tips I've picked up over the years.

# How Can I Help Someone Having a Seizure?

**Absence seizure:**

- You can't do much during an absent seizure; just stay with them until they come around.
- When they come out of it, catch them up on anything they may have missed and check if they are okay.

**Partial seizure:**

- Make sure the person is in a safe place with no restrictions around their neck and a clear space around them.
- Stay with the person; sometimes they may try to walk around, so try to keep them safe by sitting them down.
- Speak calmly and remind them that you are there for them and that they are okay. There may be times during the seizure that they can still hear you, so always assume they can and remain calm and reassuring.
- If they are jerking, do NOT hold them down or try to stop it. This can be painful for them and make the seizure worse. It's best just to let it happen.

## Tonic-clonic (full-body) seizure:

- Try to turn the person on to their side, as they may choke on saliva. Check that their airways aren't obstructed.
- Make sure the person is in a safe place with no restrictions around their neck and a clear space around them. Move away any furniture or anything that might injure them. Only move them if they are in a dangerous place – for example, on the stairs, in the road or somewhere else where they are at risk.
- I know it's scary to watch, but try your best to stay calm.
- Speak calmly and remind them that you are there for them and that they are okay. There may be times during the seizure that they can still hear you, so always assume they can and remain calm and reassuring.
- Do not let people crowd them.
- Do NOT restrain them.
- Put something soft under their head so they don't hurt themselves.
- If you are with them when the seizure starts, check the time straight away. If the seizure goes on for too long with no signs of slowing down, you may need to call a doctor for help. If they are epileptic, the time to call for help is usually after more than five minutes. However, for non-epileptic seizures, only call emergency services if their breathing is impaired or the seizure is different in nature, or much longer than usual.

- Use a tissue to wipe away any saliva.
- They will not choke on their tongue – do not put anything in their mouth.
- Minimise embarrassment – sometimes a person having a tonic-clonic seizure may wet themselves. Do not panic and deal with this as discreetly as you can; maybe cover them with a coat or blanket.
- When the seizure stops, remind them of where they are and remain calm. They may continue feeling confused or disoriented for a while after the seizure.
- They may recover fine or they may need to sleep. If they do, get them to a quiet dark place and allow them to recover.

For those of you reading this who suffer from seizures, embrace them! That may sound strange, but seizures are out of our control. I know that's a scary thing, but don't waste your time feeling beaten by them – you are strong, and resilient, don't let them win! You've got this!

If you suffer with non-epileptic seizures in particular, and have struggled especially with discrimination, I want you to know that I'm listening. I believe you and I think you're doing amazing.

If you don't suffer from seizures, then I hope this has opened your eyes a little to the pressures of living with them.

# Adjusting and Accepting

As I've said in the last chapter, the seizures starting was life-changing for me; it was a brand-new disability I had to learn to adapt to and live with. Many things changed. I already didn't have much independence because of my mental health making me a risk to myself, but now I had even less and needed constant monitoring at home in case I had another seizure.

Things changed drastically at college. When we realised the seizures weren't going anywhere, I was put on '1:1'. This means I had to have a member of the support staff with me at all times. I had gone from being a silent girl who was probably barely noticeable, to someone who was high maintenance for staff and needed constant attention. I hated feeling like such a burden. Even now, because my case of Tourette's is quite severe, I feel like I am still high maintenance for my parents and family. However, back in college, I was more of a challenge to deal with. My behaviour was fine – I wasn't noisy or disruptive in lessons at all – but my seizures were difficult to handle; they were violent, and sometimes it was my seizures that disrupted the lessons. I cringe a bit thinking about it because the feeling of being a burden is really horrible.

I was lucky I was given such a lovely 1:1, though. She had a brilliant personality; she was smiley and I remember she always carried around a giant packet of sweets in her bag. She ended up being my 1:1 for at least a year and a half. When I first met her, I didn't say a word. She could make me smile, but I couldn't bring myself to speak to her; and, at this time, I hadn't spoken to a member of staff before, or if I had, it was only a word or two.

My 1:1 sometimes changed; the staff were on a rota so they could switch around on different days. I could totally understand this, because being with me all day must have been a lot of work for them. I really was a bit of a nuisance. I didn't mean to be, but my seizures just didn't go away and they could attack at any time. But I always looked forward to days that I spent with this special 1:1. I probably didn't show it very well because I was so reserved and quiet. As the months passed, my connection with her grew stronger. She was the best out of my 1:1s at noticing the warning signs of my seizures, she was just amazing. Being able to spot the warning signs was important, since I struggled so much to communicate and tell people if I didn't feel right.

Me and my 1:1 tried to come up with ways I could tell someone I felt a seizure coming, without having to speak. We tried things like tapping her arm, or holding up a card.

The warning signs for my seizures were sometimes subtle; I could become daydreamy or twitchy, or seem vacant. Some seizures were totally out of the blue. I remember one afternoon in college, I was feeling odd. I sat at a table by myself and started drawing a mandala, which I did almost every day when I was there. I must have already partially gone into a seizure because when the staff came over to me, my 'mandala' was just scribbles. It looked like a six-year-old had drawn it. Staff realised something was very wrong because they knew how great my mandalas usually were. I was taken off to sit down somewhere and I went fully into a seizure. I still have the drawing, and it's scary to look at. I just can't believe I drew it. It really shows how much the brain is impaired during a seizure.

The good news was, as the months went by, my speech started to really improve. I could finally speak to my favourite 1:1. It felt so good to be able to talk to someone and have a laugh with them. It felt like a weight had been lifted.

I don't think at the time my 1:1 knew how much she helped me and how much she made a difference, but I'm hoping that if she reads this she will realise how amazing she was. I felt so safe with her, and if I felt a seizure coming, I didn't go into it feeling scared because I knew she'd take good care of me. And that's a big deal to me.

I was proud of myself for being able to speak to her. I could finally communicate if I wanted something, or even just have a general chit-chat. But then the next day the 1:1 would switch and I wouldn't be able to speak again. All my 1:1s were so lovely, but for some reason I just really clicked with that one in particular. To this day I miss her; I haven't seen her in a long time but I bet she would barely recognise me now. Not because of my physical appearance but because of my character. I was like a different person back then.

My seizures were a daily occurrence for quite a while,

which resulted in many ambulances being called at college and many needles being poked into my arm. At one stage I had bruises on the veins in my arms from having cannulas put in every day. I was really fed up; I just wanted them to go away so I could be like the rest of the students in my unit. I felt like my life was changing and I didn't like it; everything was so out of my control, even my own body.

My tics were a part of this as they were becoming more and more prominent during my college years. The good news was I finally knew what they were. During a hospital visit for other reasons in 2016, a doctor was talking to me and asking if I had any questions. I thought of those hiccup noises I made, and the head jerks, and mentioned them to him. He was the one who told me that they were tics. After that, all those years of hiccuping made so much sense, although at this point Tourette's wasn't suggested as the cause because you can have tics without having TS.

By age seventeen I began having spells of clearing my throat, hitting my chest and rapidly blinking. When I was eighteen, I had periods where my tics would suddenly escalate, and I would be clapping my hands, whistling, making weird squeaky noises, shouting 'Hey!' and 'Woo' or 'Wow!'

Now, at this point you're probably thinking, 'Surely you knew you had Tourette's now?' But tics can also be a symptom of FND, so for years we just put it down to that.

My mum bought a notebook for my 1:1s so they could write notes back and forth to each other about how I was doing and if I'd had any seizures that day and how long it lasted – that sort of thing.

On 4 December 2017, my mum wrote:

> Evie has had a good weekend with no
> seizures but has developed a strange
> head twitch which seems to be happening
> frequently. It doesn't lead to a seizure
> or anything else but she does find it
> frustrating.

To which my 1:1 replied:

> *Thanks for letting us know about the twitch, which is
> very regular. I also noticed she is clearing her throat
> regularly too.*

It seems so strange to look back on, because we had no idea this was actually my Tourette's starting to rear its ugly head. I had no idea that years later I'd have the whole package – swearing, throwing things, hitting, biting, shouting out rude words, yelling, screaming, all of it. It makes me sound naughty but I'm really not! It's just my pesky nonidentical twin.

# A Moment to Reflect

There were days I enjoyed at college with my lovely 1:1, with Chloe, or up with the animals. But I cannot stress enough how debilitating it was that my seizures could just randomly pop up and decide to ruin the moment. It felt like so much was happening with my body and my mind couldn't keep up. But I want to say this loudly for the people in the back:

In the long run, things do get better.

I say that truthfully and I mean it.

Sadly, depression pulls you into a horrific place and makes you think you'll be stuck there for ever. If you, reading this, are currently in that place, I know it's easy for me to sit here and say that it will get better, I understand that. I don't know how to say it so you believe it, but I cross my heart that you won't always feel like this.

What I found really important to hold on to during the rough times were things I'd achieved. Even if I couldn't appreciate them properly at the time, they gave me a glimmer of pride and hope. Despite the difficulties I've faced, I have achieved some incredible things that I will treasure for ever.

One of these moments, a month after becoming British champions again, was being asked by my gymnastics coach to perform at the ceremony for the 2012 Olympic torch relay! I wish I'd known at the time how much of a big deal this was, but I hadn't quite turned twelve yet so I knew that it was amazing, but it just felt like another performance.

Only a small number of us from my group were selected, so I felt honoured. And we were performing with the elite group, which was incredible, but at the time I found them pretty scary!

Me and another girl from my group were picked to perform a duet in the routine. This was because we were both lucky enough to have a natural flexibility, which meant we could bend ourselves into all sorts of positions.

I was also fortunate enough to have my own special moment, performing an extremely bendy move with two older girls from the elite group who were my bases for that day. It made me feel so proud of myself that I had a standout part in the routine.

During the move, the two bases had to hold my right foot and support my knee, and my left leg came over my head. (Gymnastics moves are incredibly hard to describe – I've tried my best!) So, during this, while my bottom knee was being supported, it was also bending the wrong way. This wasn't the base's fault at all; I actually have hypermobility anyway, but this move really emphasised it!

The day of the Olympic torch relay was so thrilling. Twist and Pulse from Britain's Got Talent were also performing.

I watched these two when they were on the show, and I loved them. They were a street dance act, and they were so lovely and genuine. I had my picture taken with them – I was beaming!

The weather actually turned while we were performing – rain started pouring down. Luckily for us, the stage was sheltered, so the rain didn't affect us, but it was still pretty blooming cold!

Some of my neighbours and people from my school were in the crowd, and as we all went into the starting positions waiting for the music to start, I heard loud voices shouting, 'Go on, Evie!!' Despite the cold and the rain, I was ecstatic.

That day was honestly one of the proudest times for me in all my years doing gymnastics. It was just a beautiful moment, the music playing, hearing everyone cheer as I did that special move, it was incredible, and all the other gymnasts I performed with were brilliant too. That day will be special to me for as long as I live; I'm grateful to my gym coach Katie for picking me and giving me a once-in-a-lifetime experience.

I'm hoping this will give you a bit of hope, to know that you could go through the roughest of times and still achieve amazing things, especially if you have a disability – it doesn't stop you! I'm still struggling to process the fact that I've actually written a book! And it doesn't matter how few you think your achievements are, I know you have some. Dig deep into the past, remember the feeling that it gave you at the time, and imagine how good it will feel in the future when you find that feeling again. It's waiting for you.

If I could write a letter to my seventeen-year-old self, who was in that numbing place, this is what I'd say:

Dear Evie Meg,

I'm so sorry you are feeling like this. I won't lie to you: things are going to get even worse before they get better. But I promise, they will get better eventually!

Please remember to keep opening up to Mum or Dad, you shouldn't go through this by yourself, and if you try to, things will only get worse for you. I know you feel lonely right now, but there are other people who are experiencing similar things to you – you're going to find them and they're going to lift you up. Don't lose sight of all the things in your life that you love: your family, your friends, your pets. There is joy all around you and there are exciting things waiting for you once you're ready for them. And everything you've been through so far means you have the strength to get through the next part; you can do anything!

I will see you very soon. Keep holding on!

Evie Meg x

# Is This Real?

While my mental health was still rubbish at college, my depression didn't feel as awful as it did at secondary school, so that was a positive. I felt like I had more friends than ever; Eve was still a big part of my life, I loved spending more time with Peter, and seeing Chloe at college was really lifting my mood. However, during this time I started to develop the strangest feeling I have ever experienced.

I was in a constant state of wondering, 'Where am I? Am I dreaming?' and I'm really hoping I can get across to you just how strange this felt. It didn't just feel strange, though, it was terrifying. It got so bad that I was beginning to wonder if my family was real. I was unsure if planet earth was real, and the whole concept of it just baffled me. It felt like none of the objects around me were real. That table isn't real, my bed isn't real, our house isn't real. Can you imagine feeling this 24/7?

When I looked down at my hands, they didn't look like

they belonged to me. It felt as though I was in someone else's body. I would look at family photos or pictures on my phone and I would stare at myself intensely. I just couldn't recognise myself. It was like flipping through pictures of someone else's life. It was awful, scary and so surreal.

I think my mum began to notice that I was acting a little off, and I decided I really needed to tell someone how I was feeling. I mustered enough courage one evening to tell her, and invited her into my room to talk about it. Even this felt strange because I felt like I was chatting to someone who wasn't real.

'What's going on?' Mum said to me while patting the bed to get me to sit down next to her.

'I don't feel like things around me are real, I feel like I'm dreaming.' I said this so nervously because it's always difficult opening up about feelings. I got a little upset because I was feeling so horrible.

I was really scared because I had never heard of anyone feeling like this before, and I had never experienced anything like it. After our chat my mum gave me a hug and left me alone for a bit to cool off. I started tidying my room, just to try to take my mind off all the thoughts swirling around in my head.

I was putting socks in my drawer when she came in with her iPad in her hand, and asked, 'Is this what you're feeling?'

She handed me the iPad. It was open on a webpage called mayoclinic.org and I saw a title that read 'Derealisation Disorder'.

There was a list of the symptoms, to quote a couple:

- Feelings of being alienated or unfamiliar with your surroundings, for example like you're living in a movie or a dream.
- Feeling emotionally disconnected from people you care about, as if you were separated by a glass wall.

Also, further down the page was another condition linked to derealisation, called depersonalisation disorder. This is very similar to DR, but instead of feeling disconnected from the world, and that things around you aren't real, you feel disconnected from yourself and your reflection.

'Yes, that's it!' I cried out. I couldn't believe what I was reading.

I told her I related to all of that, and I was so shocked that there was an actual name for it. I had never related to something I'd read so much before. I was happy to have a name for it because I was starting to feel like I might be slightly insane.

These symptoms can also be a passing manifestation linked to anxiety, but when they stick around for months or years, that's when they are classed as derealisation disorder or depersonalisation disorder. It took a while to be diagnosed, because although it's more common than you'd think, not a lot of doctors or psychiatrists had even heard of it.

My DR was much worse than my DP. I did feel disconnected from myself, but the sensation of the whole world being fake was overwhelming. It was much more severe than my depression and anxiety had ever been, and it took everything to a whole new level.

I started acting recklessly because I thought, 'If the world is fake and nothing is real, I can do whatever I want.'

It was an awful time, even worse than when I was at secondary school. Some mornings I woke up expecting to be back in reality, but nope, I was still stuck in this 'fake place'.

Over time it just got worse and worse. I became really poorly and no longer recognised my family. I felt like I was living in the same fake house as four strangers. They were of course my mum, my dad and my brothers, but I had no clue who they were. I also believed our pets were fake. This was heart-breaking to me because I adore animals and my pets meant the world to me.

I sat with Lottie and Beano on the bed, I kissed them on the head and said quietly, 'I don't know if you are real, but I love you.'

Looking back on this it really was a sign of the times. It just shows how unwell and out of it I was.

Mum had to keep reminding me that she gave birth to me, and that she remembers that day so she was definitely my mum! My parents were amazing during this time. I mean, they've never been anything but amazing, but this was something that was so new to all of us and they were always fighting my corner.

This is such a difficult time to write about, so I am really proud of myself for opening up about it. On my social media I have only ever touched very lightly on this disorder, so this will be the first time I've ever talked about it in detail.

I began describing the way I was feeling as 'trippy' and, because of my style, my mum started calling me her 'trippy hippie'. That is in fact where my social media name 'This Trippy Hippie' comes from!

One particular evening, like always, me and my family were sitting around the table for dinner. I sat quietly not saying a word and slowly ate my meal. I looked around and realised I had no idea who I was sitting with. I glared at my family members trying to figure things out in my head. I was at the table with all the people I love so dearly around me, but I felt like I was the only person in the room. They weren't real so they weren't actually there.

This disorder started to affect me at college. It set my selective mutism back too, and I became even quieter than before. I was still only saying a couple of words a day, but when the DR hit, I went back to saying nothing at all and I was so withdrawn. I saw no point in joining in or doing any work because it was all just 'fake'. I struggled greatly to grip on to reality and keep myself present.

Sadly, after two and a half years of doing that animal care course, my physical and mental health made it too difficult to keep going. My seizures were ruining it for me – I liked my support staff a lot but, as you can imagine, I was eighteen years old and I just wanted to be like all my other classmates. While I needed two grown-ups with me at all times (due to the severity of my seizures staff were unable to deal with them on their own, so after a year or so my 1:1 was changed to 2:1) it's not what I wanted.

My seizures were really holding me back from being able to enjoy the course, and my mental health was appalling. I was crying before and after college most days.

I don't know if I will use this course in the future, especially since my Tourette's has blown me off track! However, I do know that animals help decrease my Tourette's greatly, so if I wanted to work with animals sometime in the upcoming years I could, and I would have the experience.

If you are struggling with derealisation and/or depersonalisation disorder, here are a few things that may be helpful.

- **Find others like you:** Reaching out online and searching for other people with DP/DR really clarifies for you that this is a mental illness and it's your brain making you feel this way. If you are on Facebook, there are so many groups out there that you can join, where everyone can freely share their feelings and everyone can relate to each other.

- **Do NOT bottle it up!** This is literally one of the worst things you can do – most people learn this the hard way. Our feelings are like a can of fizzy lemonade; if we are shaken up with anxieties, stresses and worries, we start to bubble inside. We don't release these tensions anywhere and so we eventually explode. Learning to speak to someone you feel comfortable with when you can feel things fizzing up is vital for recovery. It can be hard, but I promise it will feel like such a weight off your shoulders. You shouldn't have to carry all that around by yourself. It almost feels like when you've been needing a wee all day, and when you finally have one it feels so good!

- **Think logically:** Give yourself reminders of things that, logically, must be real. Perhaps it's a plant you've cared for since it was a little seedling, or an animal you've had since it was tiny. Focus on something you've had since before you started feeling like this.

- **Use your senses:** Go outside and feel the sun's rays on your face. You feel that lovely warmth? That's no trickery, that's not fake. Or put headphones in and listen to music as loud as your ears can take it. Drown out the world for a bit and feel the vibrations of the song. If you put on a really great track that you love, you may even get goosebumps – that's not fake. Look at the hairs standing up on your arms and all the little bumps.

- **Be gentle with yourself:** Everything feels so fake and dreamy, I get it. You are fragile at the moment, and that's okay; it just means you need to be kind to yourself. Don't push yourself into situations you know you might struggle with. If you can't go and meet your friends, that's okay. If you need a day off work or school, that's okay. Take the day to watch your favourite movies, stuff your face with tasty food or have a good cry in the shower if you need to.

Reflect on this battle you're fighting and notice how strong you are. You're doing great. You've got this!

# I'm Not Crazy

I was worried that if you read this next chapter, you might see me differently. But while it may be difficult to explain and share, I'm determined to break the stigma of delusions and mental illness. I want to open your minds to other people who may have delusions or might struggle so much to grasp on to reality.

While me believing the world was fake was a delusion in itself, I developed other odd beliefs. I have always had stuffed toys in my bedroom; there's never been a single day in my life when my room has been without a teddy. They never gave me any issues; they were a huge source of comfort to me.

But when I was poorly, my mindset changed completely. Looking back, this really shows me just how unwell I was. My teddies all have glass eyes, and I well and truly believed that there were cameras in their eyes watching me. This made me feel so unsafe in my own room, and whenever I changed my clothes I turned all my teddies around so they faced the wall. Even my sweet bear Popcorn, who I have loved so much all my life, was now a source of paranoia.

My room is my safe space, it's somewhere I go for alone

time, to meditate, to light candles and do my art, but now it had turned into something entirely different and to me this felt cruel.

I believe this was one of my first delusions, but, after this, I gained a lot more. In our bathroom we have a small ceiling fan, and I was convinced this also had a camera in it. I began showering with a towel over the shower screen, so 'no one could see me'. This became a habit, and I continued to shower like this for at least a year. It was actually something I worked through in therapy later on, and I now shower freely!

The thing about delusions is that it's no good telling someone with delusions 'it's not true' because we are fully convinced that it is. I know people have good intentions when they say that, and it's just an automatic response, because if I went up to you and said, 'There're cameras in my teddy bear's eyes and they're watching me', you'd probably be thinking, 'What the f—' and then say something like, 'No there's not, there's nothing there.' Which is okay, it just won't change my mind at all.

What can sometimes help is, if possible, giving us proof that it's not real. And telling us that we are safe. I never got sick of hearing my parents tell me, 'It's okay, Evie, you're safe.' Even if a lot of times I didn't feel like I was, it was still nice to hear it.

I think people who don't know much about this topic may think that if we are simply told that our delusions aren't real, we will snap out of it and be fine. The truth is that it doesn't work like that. I wish it did. But delusions can stick around for days, weeks, months or even years. Mine lasted for years, but the severity waxed and waned, meaning I had periods where it didn't affect me too much.

After leaving college, they still burdened me, but while I didn't believe there were cameras in my teddies any more, I now thought that out there on lamp posts, shop windows, anywhere like that, were posters of me with my face and description on. That people were searching for me as if I was on a wanted list. I believed this with my whole heart and it was terrifying. I didn't like going for walks and, when we did, I kept my head down whenever a car drove past in case the driver recognised me from the 'posters'. I felt unsafe outside, and even in my own home.

During a truly awful time of paranoia and delusions in 2019, I was stuck in an episode that lasted a few weeks and almost had me sent to hospital. It was one of the worst times of my life. I had never been in such a state.

I was in the living room one evening with my mum, and I suddenly got it into my head that there were men outside the living-room windows waiting for me and coming to get me. I started crying, panicking and yelling inconsolably. Mum tried to comfort me but I was convinced they were there.

At this time, we had just got a new puppy, Teddy. He was only a few months old at this point. Later the same evening as the meltdown in the living room, I was upstairs, and I was staying in Mum's room at night with her because I was so mentally unwell. All of a sudden I started crying, saying that the 'men' were now in the house and they were trying to take Teddy. Anything to do with animals and I was heartbroken – I thought someone was taking away my sweet puppy. Once again I was sobbing, so Mum called downstairs to my dad and asked him to bring Teddy upstairs so I could see that he was perfectly fine.

Less than a minute later, Dad appeared at the door with Teddy in his arms. Teddy was so tiny and fluffy; he looked at me with his puppy eyes as Dad handed him to me to have a cuddle with him in bed. I immediately stopped crying and my breathing settled down. His soft fur and puppy smell were exactly what I needed.

Even when I was embracing Teddy, I never thought, 'Oh, I was freaking out for no reason, there were never any men downstairs' because in the moment I thought it was as real as anything. I was clueless that the delusions I was having were just that. Delusions.

This period was probably the hardest thing we went through as a family. I sometimes heard my brother coming down the stairs and thought it was a strange man coming for me, so yet again Mum had to calm me down. I can't imagine what this must have been like for them as parents.

Mum took me for a doctor's appointment to discuss how I was. That's when being put into a psychiatric hospital was mentioned. I was so unaware of reality that I thought this doctor's office, this building and the doctor himself weren't real. So believing this I got up, went to the door and tried to leave. My mum stopped me but it's like having someone else's memories, it's so out of character for me.

Written by Mum:

> Evie became so unwell and delusional at one point we thought she'd be admitted. It was the worst time of my life. She didn't know who we were and would say, 'Don't lie to me, you're not my mum.' She would be terrified of her brothers and totally believe we lived in a fake world where everything and everyone was either

a dream or some sort of fake creation.
She didn't even look like herself.
She never smiled, her mouth was set
in a strange clench and her eyes, her
beautiful smiling eyes, were just dead,
nothing there. It was heart-breaking to
see our little girl, who had always been
known for her smile and bubbly nature,
so broken. We honestly felt like we were
losing her.

  I had to spend twenty-four hours with
her for months to keep her safe. It was
exhausting. Not because of the intensive
care needed but because of the fear. The
fear of not being able to pull her back
to us or that she'd lost her fight.

I'm not ashamed to say that in the past I was delusional.
It's a word with a lot of stigma attached to it; it makes
us sound insane, crazy, like we're losing the plot. It's not
true. Individuals with delusions are just people who have
lost themselves; they have lost reality and need help; they
need people to stick with them until their real self resurfaces again.

We all love a happy ending, and I can now proudly say
that I have been delusion-free for at least two years now. My
symptoms of DP and DR have reduced massively, and no
longer impact my daily life. I typed that with a big smile on
my face! This is a huge accomplishment.

I've kept a diary since I was ten years old, and during my
time battling derealisation I wrote entries expressing the
awful feelings of fakeness I had. I had struggled through

anxiety, depression, seizures and much more, yet I wrote in my diary that I believed DR was going to be the disorder that tipped me over the edge. Some people have DR mildly, but for me I was barely functioning anymore. I honestly thought that although I had fought through so much, derealisation was going to be the thing that was just too much for me to handle.

Yes, I had to fight, and luckily I was never fighting alone, but I did it. I worked so hard to get through it, and, with the help of medication and therapy, I have recovered from derealisation and depersonalisation disorder, and I no longer have any delusions. The sixteen-, seventeen-year-old me never thought I'd be able to say that!

I am in a better headspace than I have ever been. Excuse my language, but I am so f**king proud of myself! Thank goodness it's over.

I thought long and hard about whether I was ready to share with the world that part of what I went through. The delusions are something only a small number of people know about. Well, I guess not anymore!

I decided to include it in my book, because I once believed that I was never going to come out of that state. I thought I was going to be stuck in a constant headspace of fear, paranoia, danger and emptiness.

If I can prove to at least one person that recovery IS possible, then it was worth it.

Written by Mum:

> The turning point came in 2019 when,
> with the right medication, an amazing
> therapist who we found privately and

an abundance of love, she started to recover. There had been some reckless choices and self-destructive behaviour through the months and they started to play on her mind. Her derealisation was much less, easing with the medication. She knew we were her family again and felt guilty, and with that came a want to recover and live life again. She slowly started to come back, her smile was there more, her eyes sparkling again. She began to find her voice and speak more freely about everything she'd gone through. She's always had amazing friends and they were there for her. Peter was always there, taking her out for walks and picnics; Eve, Rachel and Chloe all keeping in touch regularly, checking in with her and supporting her.

She was still having seizures and other health problems during all this time and started to use her social media channels as a way to express herself and talk about her health. It was an amazing outlet for her. She found others with FND, others with derealisation, depression and mental health problems. She's always been an empath; she cares too much about people and animals, she worries for them more than herself. She found that by opening up about her mental health and raising awareness around it, others connected with her, were helped by it, reached out to her.

I will never forget what Evie's been through and hope she never faces those difficulties again, but I believe going through it has made her into a little warrior. She faced the worst of times at an incredibly young age, has come out of it fighting and is determined to help others in the Tourette's and FND community.

# Living the Dream

In late 2019, I found myself not a college student, not working, and in far better health than I'd been previously. I was of course still having seizures but they were fairly under control, and while I had frequent headaches, I kept them at bay with paracetamol. My tics weren't too bad either, which meant I could find something new to do. That's when I enrolled on a teaching assistant course. I have always adored children, and from a very young age I knew I wanted to work with either animals or children when I was older.

That September, I started placement in my old primary school, where I had previously been and met Naomi. I was so pumped about this! I'd recovered from DP, DR; I wasn't having delusions and my depression was under control, so I was thrilled that I'd be able to really put my everything into this course.

I was incredibly nervous on my first day. The last time I was there was during my home-schooling days, but now I was here professionally. It felt so strange to be the adult!

I was working in early years, the reception classroom (where the children are four or five), and the teacher I worked with was so lovely. Before long I was working with groups of children by myself – I felt so grown-up! That's not to say it wasn't a little scary. I've struggled all my life with being able to process things quickly, such as picking up my gymnastics routines or answering questions during my counselling sessions. When I was fifteen or so I was told after being tested that I had a longer than average processing time, so being a little 'slow' sometimes affected me when I was with the children.

My memory loss, however, which I have as a result of my FND, was a right pain in the backside too, affecting me in class more than my processing problem. The kids were great about it. I told them I was like Dory, from the Disney film *Finding Nemo*, as she has short-term memory loss, and this helped them understand better. They were so sweet, and often helped me remember things.

I recall sitting with them in groups round a table and they'd have to say, 'You've already done me, miss!' since I wouldn't remember which children I'd already had in my groups. It was lovely to see them be so understanding.

The teacher would sometimes ask me to make copies of something down at the printer, so I'd say, 'Yes, of course!' The primary school is only small, so from reception class down the corridor to the printer in the office was only forty seconds away really. But when I'd arrive at the printer . . . I'd realise I couldn't remember what she had asked for. There were a few occasions when I'd have to go back up and ask again, which made me feel so silly. Once I'd realised that my brain wasn't letting me remember, I began walking to the printer mumbling, 'Twenty-five copies in colour, twenty-five copies in colour', over and over so I wouldn't forget!

I made great connections with the children; I was absolutely loving being there. One child in particular would give me daily compliments. 'I like your hair, ooh, I like your top, and I like your scarf' – it was too cute! Instant confidence boost! During lunchtimes I'd also see if I could quickly say hello to Naomi and Yasmin.

While I was only actually in school once a week – the rest of the days were spent on written work at home, not as good but has to be done! – I loved being in the classroom so much. I loved being greeted by the kids and seeing their smiles; I loved working with them. It was just everything I wanted.

I was so proud. I really felt like I was finally heading in the right direction and where I wanted to be.

# Return of the Tics!

In early spring 2020 (the dreaded year of Covid-19!), after being quiet for so long, my tics became more noticeable again. For example, my arms would suddenly extend, accompanied by the head jerks, and I kept making a sniffing sound. This carried on through to May, when things really took a turn for the worse.

On 17 May, my family and I went for a walk by a river. I was in a really good mood that day; in fact, I was hyper, which now I know isn't always a good thing when you have Tourette's. I had so much energy in my body on that walk; I was jumping and skipping around, and I could feel my tics getting worse. As we carried on, I realised I was actually finding it difficult to walk because of all the tics that were happening. My tics were just firing out constantly, my arms moving, my neck jerking backwards, and I shouted 'Hey!' at some poor fisherman. Along the way I had to sit down on a rock with my mum to try to calm down.

I was exhausted when the tics calmed down, and it was

literally that day when I started wondering if they were more than FND tics, and I think my parents did too. I remember saying to my mum, 'I wonder if this is what people mean when they talk about "tic attacks"?'

## What Are Tic Attacks?

Tic attacks are something I dread, possibly more than my seizures. A tic attack is an episode of an outburst of tics all at once. Everyone's tic attacks are different, some lasting five to ten minutes, others lasting hours and hours.

The feeling of it is difficult to describe to someone who doesn't have Tourette's, but usually I say that it feels like I've been electrocuted, and there's electricity in my veins pumping around my body. It's a horrible feeling that doesn't go away until the tic attack is over.

My tic attacks are usually different every time. I've had some when I just can't sit still, and I have that electric feeling mostly in my legs. During those episodes my tics cause me to jump around, and my mum has to clear the area so I don't get hurt.

Once I had a tic attack where I couldn't stop screaming. My throat felt red raw but I just couldn't stop. My lovely dog Teddy was worried about me and climbed on my knee, which was an amazing thing for him to do since my screaming would have been deafening to him.

One of my most severe tic attacks was on 8 September 2020. It started when I was sitting at my desk, doing stuff on my computer. I had my legs crossed and my knee kept jumping up and banging against the desk, while at the same time my head was flinging backwards. This happened over and over again. My parents could hear the banging and came in to check on me.

My mum helped me off my chair and laid me down on my bed. It didn't take long till I went into a full-blown tic attack. My breathing was being compromised by my tics, and I couldn't stop moving – my arms were thrashing out to the side, my hand banging off my bedroom wall. My mum tried building a buffer of cushions against the wall to protect my hand, but I was moving so much that all the cushions kept falling. We struggled to get a diazepam down me (this is my emergency medication), but even that wasn't calming the attack, which is unusual as it normally has an effect in minutes. This attack was too strong.

Eventually an ambulance had to be called. They were so lovely, but they couldn't do anything to help as this wasn't like my seizures. If it was a seizure, they'd put a cannula in my arm and give me medication to calm it, but putting a cannula into someone with Tourette's who's having a tic attack would be virtually impossible. So we just waited it out.

When the attack finally subsided, my poor hand was swollen and red. The paramedics were worried that it was broken, and that all the adrenaline from the attack was masking the pain. So I was taken to hospital with them for an X-ray. I had to go by myself because of Covid-19, and that was the first time I have ever been through hospital tests alone. It was scary and nerve-racking, since for the majority of my life I have had to have someone with me wherever I go in case I have a seizure.

During the time I was in the hospital, the bruising started to come out and my hand looked terrible. I was also feeling the after-effects of the tic attack and all my muscles were super-heavy, as if they had weights in them.

During the X-ray I had to hold in my tics so my hand wouldn't jerk. This is called suppressing. Suppressing isn't really recommended as it can be harmful and may lead to a tic attack later. However, in certain situations, such as having an X-ray, it needs to be done. The feeling is not nice. When I suppress my tics, I can feel tingling and itching going through my limbs – this is the feeling of them wanting to tic. This night, though, I had been given medication to try to calm the attack, so I was calmer than usual and managed okay for the X-ray.

While I was waiting for the results, I sat back in the waiting room. Luckily it wasn't too busy, but it was bizarre seeing everyone seated away from each other; I was honestly scared I was going to catch Covid in there.

Sat two seats away from me was an old man; he must have been in his mid-eighties. He was on his own and looked so bored. After contemplating for a while and building up the courage, I spoke to him and asked him if he was okay. I wish I had better recall so I could tell you what we talked about. I know I asked him if he had any pets at home, and I showed him a photo of my dog Teddy; I vaguely remember him telling me a story about a dog. Bless him, it was hard for him to understand me through our masks, and I felt bad but I couldn't take it off. I was so proud, though – for talking to a stranger when I was alone, and I initiated it too! I've never really done that before. I'd come a long way from my selective mutism at college!

Eventually I was called in for my X-ray results. They said they were worried about a hairline fracture but luckily no bones were broken. I sent my parents a text with the good news. Dad came and picked me up and I went home for a sleep, as by this time it was the early hours of the morning.

Sometimes my FND and my Tourette's mix together at the same time and I hate it. I was watching TV with my mum one evening when I noticed my tics were getting more severe and I realised I was having another attack. However, this attack was different. I was having lots of dystonic tics (this is where the muscles lock for a certain amount of time and you can't move them until they unlock – for example, an arm stretching out, or a hand going into a claw shape) and I was in so much pain because my muscles were contracting all the time and going into funny shapes. As the attack went on, I ended up with my whole body being fully stiff and I couldn't move anything. My mum tried moving my arms and legs but I was like a wooden doll. It was so bizarre but clearly an FND symptom. My entire body started heating up and it felt like I was on fire. I had to hold back tears until my muscles started to release.

After a while, my legs relaxed, and my neck, my stomach muscles unclenched, my toes uncurled, and my arms relaxed too. Yet my hands were stuck clenched in fists for around half an hour afterwards, caused again by my FND. So having Tourette's syndrome and FND attacks at the same time can be agonising.

It was also around this time I swore for the first time – the coprolalia tic I mentioned earlier! I was in the back garden with Peter, playing with Teddy. It was June so the weather was so lovely.

My tics were active that day, and a bee buzzed past me, skimming my face. Straight away I suddenly said, 'F**king bee.' I put my hands over my mouth and looked at Peter. I couldn't believe that had just come out my mouth. I knew about the swearing tic and was dreading it, hoping I just wouldn't develop coprolalia. I felt upset with myself and Peter reassured me and helped me feel better.

I had my phone recording at the time as I wanted to share with everyone on social media what my tics were like. However, I was so mortified that I'd sworn without meaning to that I deleted the footage.

I remember very clearly how awful I felt; I thought about it all evening. Swearing isn't the end of the world, but when it's involuntary, it's frightening. Now I have adjusted to having coprolalia. I don't like it, at all, but I don't feel horrible about myself just for swearing anymore.

With my tics in full swing and clearly not going away anytime soon, Mum and I had to talk to the head teacher and tell her that I couldn't come into school anymore on the teaching assistant course. I was completely heartbroken. I never got to properly say bye to the kids because, as I left, Covid-19 struck and all schools were closed. I was so angry with my brain. Things were going so amazingly for me but my brain had thrown something else at me to completely ruin it.

I couldn't have continued at school with my tics the way they were/are. I might have sworn in the classroom, I might have thrown something. My tics – even when just noises – can be loud sometimes and I didn't want to startle the kids. If I'd had a tic attack at school it just wouldn't have been possible to manage in that environment. I was hoping maybe it was just a flare-up of my tics – which is what had happened back in 2018 – but months and months passed and every day they were the same.

I felt absolutely crushed. At one point during 2020, I received a certificate in the post saying I was now a Level 2 qualified teaching assistant. I wanted to cry when I opened it. I haven't looked at it since, it's too hard. I keep trying to remind myself of everything I have still achieved since then. I mean, look, I've written a book!

So, with me now swearing, involuntarily blurting out full sentences, having violent tic attacks, the whole package, we all knew these weren't FND tics. The tics were becoming unmanageable at times and we knew something had to be done. Pretty soon after they became severe, Mum wanted to speak to a doctor as my tics had never been like this before. We were all shocked and it was affecting the whole family, not just me.

My brothers tried to watch TV and I was shouting uncontrollably, drowning out the programme. At dinner times my family had food thrown at them and the table would sometimes shift if I had a sudden violent tic. Family walks weren't the same anymore, as I might have tic attacks or tics that dropped me to the floor on my knees.

It wasn't easy for any of us, we were all struggling and wanted answers.

In October 2020, after many, many tic attacks, injuries and difficult days, I was finally diagnosed with Tourette's. I had to go to a private neurologist because the waiting list on the poor NHS was ridiculously long and we didn't want to wait. My family and I knew I had Tourette's, but we wanted the official diagnosis so I could get proper help, perhaps try medication; it also meant I had a name to tell people.

Being diagnosed and hearing the neurologist say the words "Tourette's syndrome" was so strange and caused so many emotions. I'd known for some time that I had TS, but I had been trying not to think about it because it's for life. Whereas a tic disorder can pass. This upset me at first but I have adjusted to it now. I was having a bit of a pity party when I decided that enough was enough. Yes, I have a lifelong disability and that sucks, but what am I going to do, be miserable about it as long as I live? Doesn't sound very appealing. That's when I started to have a better attitude towards the new diagnosis and my mindset changed. Bring it on!

I now see it as a positive. It's a great feeling to have a name for my condition, which means I can easily tell people, 'I have Tourette's', if I need to. This usually happens in shops or restaurants. We went for a lovely meal for my mum's birthday in October 2020 – my tics were in full swing that day! I swore at the lovely lady serving us, so Mum said, 'Sorry, she's got Tourette's!' We all laughed and the lady said, 'Oh, that's okay!' with a big smile on her face. Usually, once people know, they are totally fine and can often have a laugh with us.

It's a shame that my tics had to get so severe for me to be diagnosed, but we got there eventually!

What people don't realise about individuals with TS is that we can do virtually everything that everyone else can do. We can have successful jobs, have our own family, some of us can drive, do sports (and be pretty amazing at it too!).

My plans for my future have changed a lot. Of course, I was desperate to work in a school with young children, but I have realised I don't need to be in a school to make a difference in a child's life.

In early 2021, I was on TikTok when an account caught my attention. It showed videos of a little girl having the roughest of times. This was twelve-year-old Teagan, who lives with severe epilepsy, cerebral palsy, autism and a chromosome disorder. She has the most severe case of epilepsy some doctors have ever seen, but she often has a beautiful big smile on her face. I saw that Teagan needs medicinal cannabis oil just to get through the day, and that her mum Emma was fundraising to help pay for the expensive monthly cost of the oil.

I couldn't watch these videos and not do anything. I began sharing her story on my social media platforms, to bring more attention, and hopefully bring in donations. Of course, I myself donated, and continued doing whatever I could to help. I'm a huge believer that if you are lucky enough to have a large online platform like me, you have to use it to do good. What better way to make the most of 13 million followers than to ask them to help you raise money for an incredibly poorly but strong little girl?

Over time I became very close with Emma. I sent gifts to their house for Teagan, and so far I have raised over $4,000, which pays for two months' worth of oil and has saved Teagan's life. (Yes, it really is $2,000 a month!)

One day someone left a comment on a video I posted of me and Teagan which really hit me quite hard. It said that I was clearly meant to work with children and, although it may be different to what I used to do, I was still having an impact on children. I never even thought of it like that until I read this comment, and I felt amazing.

Yes, I'm not working in a primary school anymore, but why did I think that would be the end of me helping kids? I never even realised I was making an impact until I saw this comment and since then I have felt so much better about myself. Giving up the primary school had left a big grey cloud hanging above my head, but it now felt as though the sun was beginning to shine.

Teagan is now like my little sister, and I finally met this

incredible girl and her mum at the end of April 2021, when we spent the loveliest weekend together. Teagan cannot talk at all, but this doesn't stop her from communicating. She leant in for kisses and adores cuddles. The amazing thing is, while I was with Teagan, or comforting her when she had seizures, my Tourette's just went away. She has as much of an impact on me as I do on her.

All of this has really been a wake-up call for me. I lost hope when I had to give up the teaching assistant course, thinking I'd end up in some job I didn't really like, unable to work with children anymore, but that's not the case at all.

It just shows that, although things may not work out how you expect them to, there are always other options, which may in fact be even better. So never lose hope!

If you are interested in Teagan's journey but cannot donate, please don't worry! You can still support her just by following her journey @helpforteagan on Instagram and Facebook, and @helpforteagan1 on TikTok. If you would like to donate, you can click the link in her Instagram bio. It is so greatly appreciated, thank you so much. <3

# My Tourette's Diary

Throughout the journey of writing this book, I've been keeping some diary entries to give you an idea of what my Tourette's and other conditions are like on a daily basis – to show you the good and bad days. Tourette's isn't the same every day; it can drastically change depending on emotions or what I'm doing. I hope you find it interesting!

**6 January 2021**

My Tourette's smashed a glass today . . . oops!

**10 January 2021**

My tics haven't been too bad today; however, for the past week or so my punching tic has been awful. I have a tic where I punch walls, only with my right hand. I usually punch it three times in a row, getting harder each time, so the last punch is the hardest. This has been so bad lately, I walk around the house wearing a padded glove. My hand is a mess, all funny shades of green, purple, pink and yellow. I am slightly worried I have a hairline fracture or that I'm causing long-term damage, but having an X-ray is a last resort, since going to hospital is such a high risk at the moment. I might have to get one in the upcoming week, though, since it hasn't changed for days. I'll keep you updated.

The trouble is, my Tourette's doesn't let it heal. So even if it is fractured or cracked, I'm still punching walls many times every day.

The feeling of it is awful. I feel the urge to do it going down my arm as if it's building up. Tonight I was trying to draw my mandalas, and that feeling down my arm was so bad I had to put my pen down and let the tic happen. I can usually distract myself but I guess it was too strong.


## 12 January 2021

Today I spent most of the day in the hospital getting an X-ray on my hand. They let my dad stay with me this time because we told them I have seizures. It's pretty crazy going to hospital during a pandemic. I felt so unclean!

During my X-ray, the nurse positioned my hand but then my Tourette's moved it away – this kept happening! But she was so lovely. The machine made a camera clicking noise and my tics said 'Smile!' which made her laugh. We waited ages and ages for the results but my hand isn't broken! Which is a relief. It doesn't make the pain any less but at least I know now.

My Tourette's also decided to say in the waiting room that the reason I was in hospital was because I have syphilis . . . (Obviously not true.)

## 16 January 2021

I have had a headache all evening; I thought maybe I was just tired. Mum and I sat down on the sofa to watch The Voice, but literally five minutes in I went into a seizure. I remember it starting – I suddenly started feeling like things were spinning and as if I was floating away. I hadn't had a seizure in a while. It was a full-body convulsion seizure and lasted five minutes. My tics started again when I was barely out of the seizure; the convulsions had stopped but Mum said I mumbled 'beans' when I was still out of it!

When I came round from the seizure I was paralysed from the neck down, I couldn't even lift my head to begin with. I could wiggle my toes first, then over the space of five minutes I had full mobility back. Thank goodness! It's scary because I never know how long the paralysis will last. Sometimes it's five minutes, sometimes it's five days.

## 23 January 2021

I hit 11 million followers today on TikTok! How amazing!

## 25 January 2021

So, I got a new tic while in Lidl today . . . It's an interesting one! I basically hiss like a cat. I pretty much walked round the shop hissing at people if they got too close to me . . .

## 31 January 2021

My tics haven't been great today. We went for a walk round our town (even though all the shops are closed) and I could feel all the tics inside my body. It's very strange – it's like when you shake a fizzy can and it's all bubbling inside. When we got home I had a big tic attack, it was horrible. My tics were screaming so much and so loud that I got a sore throat and for the rest of the evening I sounded like a man. The tics were also compromising my breathing – sometimes I hold my breath and I don't know when I'll be able to breathe again. Or I have a gasping tic where I gasp for air, which makes it look like a panic attack. I was exhausted when it finally finished. Tomorrow is a new day! (And a new month!)

## 7 February 2021

I baked some pancakes today with my mum for a YouTube video. Baking with Tourette's is always interesting . . .

While we were recording I got a pain in my head above my left eye. This is often a warning sign for a seizure, and literally twenty seconds after complaining about the pain, I had an absent seizure. Absent seizures aren't as bad as full-body ones, but they're still not nice, and can sometimes be a sign that a bigger seizure is coming. I had a few more absences after that so we had to stop recording and go for a lie-down. I don't really remember it much so I must have been pretty out of it. I had a long nap and we finished the pancakes afterwards! Mum made toffee sauce to go with them and we ate them for pudding. Yummy!

## 13 February 2021

The past twenty-four hours have been eventful. Last night I had a banging headache for over an hour. I was sort of waiting for a seizure but it was just lingering. Eventually the seizure started and I knocked on the wall for my mum. She heard me knocking and came in to sit with me. She is always so amazing when I have a seizure.

It was awful because at the beginning of the seizure I was still conscious so I could feel my eyebrows twitching and my mouth drooping but I couldn't do anything about it. Mum was so amazing and kept telling me that I was safe. I dribbled a lot during this seizure, that might be a bit TMI but seizures aren't pretty! I'm not sure how long it lasted, but when I finally came out of it, my whole body was so sore, and I knew straight away something was wrong with my mouth because my face felt funny.

My jaw had popped out of place again. I lay still for a couple of minutes to let myself recover, then Mum helped me sit up and I slowly moved my jaw around until I heard it crack and it felt more comfortable.

I cried a bit afterwards, just because that seizure was a particularly horrible one, and my body felt so rotten. I went to sleep and woke up today feeling a bit better, but then at lunchtime-ish my left hand curled up and didn't unlock for four hours. This is actually shorter than usual; sometimes this happens for a week or longer, but it's still painful and debilitating. I actually wrote the first part of this entry with one hand, but I got frustrated. I'm wearing my brace to keep my wrist straight, otherwise it gets so sore throughout the day.

It started to relax this evening when I was just resting in my room, and then my wrist and fingers relaxed too. It's much better now.

## 23 February 2021

My Tourette's isn't good at the moment. Well, it's odd because it's not actually too active, but I'm struggling to walk and stand up. I have a tic where my legs buckle and drop me to the floor, and I've had this tic for months, but it's really bad at the moment.

When I go out I have to sit in my wheelchair, otherwise I'm on the floor every few steps I take. I've cut and bruised my knees, so it's probably for the best. It has been mixing with my FND too – my hand locked up yesterday for most of the day, and I just couldn't unlock it. It kept me awake till 2am because it was sore and tingly. At least when I woke up this morning it wasn't locked anymore!

Hopefully I'll be back on my feet soon and the dropping tic will settle down.


## 28 February 2021

Yesterday was so rough. I don't want this diary to be totally negative, so I'll tell you the positive bits first. The weather has really been improving lately; the sun has actually been out more, which my animals are absolutely loving. Yesterday Mum came into my room and woke me up since it was almost midday. I couldn't believe I'd slept so long. Pretty much as soon as I sat up I went into an absent seizure which is unusual, so we knew it wasn't going to be a great day, but the weather was lovely so I sat in the garden on a picnic mat. I let my rabbits out to zoom around and Teddy was on his lead next to me, really soaking up the sun. Those moments, seeing my animals so happy, really make my heart fill with joy.

The rest of the day I continued having absence seizures but I was doing okay, I was still myself. At around 9.30pm, Mum and I were watching *The Voice* on TV. I said to my mum, 'Can you come and sit with me?' because I started feeling weird and wanted to be able to see her. My arms felt so light, like I had helium balloons tied round my wrists and they could just float off. This is a new symptom for me. It was really odd. It didn't take long for me to go into a seizure. At first I was unconscious, so I don't remember actually going into it. But then something strange happened. My brain woke up, so I was fully aware, but my body was still having a seizure. I was drooling, convulsing and my jaw was locked again. I hated this so much, I'd rather be unconscious. I couldn't speak very well but I mumbled to my mum, 'Why am I awake?' It was awful. It was as if I had gained conscious-ness too early. After a little while of still seizing, I soon fell unconscious again, and apparently this is when the seizure got even worse. My parents said I had never had convulsions like this before, which is really something because I've had all kinds of seizures since 2016.

Now thirty-five minutes had passed; by this time I had overheated, I was dripping with sweat, my breathing wasn't great and I was convulsing severely. My parents had to call an ambulance. Next thing I know, I'm still on the couch but I have a cannula in my arm and I'm super-drowsy. As expected, my jaw had dislocated again so I had to pop it back into place. They had given me diazepam to stop the seizure, which I have had many times.

They wheeled me into the ambulance and took me to hospital. I noticed that the cannula was more painful than all the other times I'd had one, and a huge lump had formed where it was put in. I'm not very squeamish, but for some reason I hated looking at it. When we got to hospital, a nurse told me that it had probably hit tissue rather than a vein, because I was convulsing so bad.

After a while of being in the monitoring room with Mum, I had another seizure, the same length but I didn't have the type of convulsions I'd had earlier. Eventually I was okay to go home. Mum and I walked out to the car park to meet Dad – I only had socks on my feet so the ground was freezing! By the time we got into bed it was 2.30 in the morning.

I've felt pretty rotten today and my arm is sore where the cannula was put in wrong; it wasn't the paramedic's fault, though, it's just something that happens sometimes. I was a bit disheartened because it's been at least a year since we've had to call an ambulance for my seizures. Onwards and upwards!

### 6 March 2021

I'm doing much better after last week. My arm still hurts from the cannula going in wrong, but I am much, much better. Hopefully tonight I can watch The Voice without any incidents! My legs aren't letting me walk too well still, but I had a really great gymnastics stretching session today.

### 17 March 2021

I have some news! I have started medication for my Tourette's for the first time ever! I have been on medication for mental health reasons for years but never for my tics. I have only been on the new meds for two days so far. The reason we've waited so long to try medication is because we were worried about how it might clash with the others I take daily, and I have been stable for a while now and didn't want anything to change that. The tablet I'm on now is also used to reduce blood pressure, which isn't great for me since I have low blood pressure anyway. So now when I stand up after sitting down for a while I have to be more careful than I used to be. The medication seems to be quite strong; it makes me drowsy and I don't know if I like that. One of my other tablets knocks me out completely but I only have to take it before bed so that's fine. However, I take this new one three times a day. Hopefully my body will adjust soon.

## 20 March 2021

Sadly, my new medication still isn't working out for me. It's messing with my blood pressure so badly, I almost passed out this morning. Just because I squatted for a second. It was scary; I was in my room and when I stood up everything started going black – luckily my bed was right in front of me so I could stop myself from falling. Afterwards I was so nauseous I sat in the garden for some air.

We are reducing the tablet to only one three times a day rather than two, to see if that makes a difference.

## 21st March 2021

A little update about the new medication: I have stopped it completely. The side-effects weren't worth it and it wasn't helping my tics anyway. It was messing with my blood pressure too much.

I'm still in a wheelchair due to my Tourette's making me fall down and hurt myself every few steps, but, on a positive note, the weather has been lovely lately so the bunnies have been running round the garden in the sun – they are loving it! It makes me so, so happy to see them enjoying themselves so much.

## 26 March 2021

These past two days have been incredible. Yesterday at 5pm I announced to my followers that I am writing a book. I am overwhelmed with love! It's been less than twenty-four hours and My Nonidentical Twin is #1 in some book categories on Amazon!!I truly can't believe it. I'm speechless. It hasn't all sunk in yet – hopefully it hits me soon!

## 29 March 2021

Difficult day with my tics today. I had an episode in the shower and scratched up all the right side of my face. It was really horrible.

My body curled over and my left hand locked, but my right hand was clawing at my face, scratching the skin off. I look as if I've had an allergic reaction.

I was crying – it was as if someone else's hand was scratching me, not mine. I couldn't stop it. My face is a mess, but it will heal quickly I hope.

I hope these diary entries have given you a good insight into how drastically things can change from one day to the next. I always wanted to be totally raw and realistic about Tourette's – sometimes it's manageable and sometimes it's terrible. Like they say, it's not about waiting for the storm to pass, it's about learning to dance in the rain!

# Riding the Storm

So that's where I am with my Tourette's, and my FND can be tricky, too. Stress can be a huge trigger for FND and it can be hard to guard against that, especially when it comes to unexpected grief. Within quick succession, my cat Beano and my rabbits Lola and Pip died, causing my depression to spiral within two months. It took me a while to process what had happened because it was so sudden and totally out of the blue.

While my brain was processing everything, it made my legs paralysed again. I was back to using a wheelchair and crutches. It sounds so dramatic, my legs being paralysed because my rabbits died, but if you own any pet, you'll know what it's like. Besides, FND is out of my control. I thought to myself that it seemed a dramatic reaction, but it's not like I could do anything about it.

Lola and Pip died of a deadly virus called VHD2, so we had to throw away everything they'd touched. Absolutely everything. It was as if they were never here and that was rough to deal with. But what I could do was look through photos of them and the time we spent together. This is really healthy for me and allows me to cry so I can begin moving forwards.

After a week or so, I regained mobility in my legs. After that incident I was worried that if anything else happened, my brain would be a big drama queen and shut down my legs. The joys of FND!

Thankfully, right now, all my animals are healthy and doing just fine. I feel as though now that my mental health is in a good place, I would cope better if anything were to happen, so hopefully that would mean there would be no paralysis!

Writing this book is a perfect example of how I coped with deadlines and expectations. I admit it has been tough. My brain has often decided to throw seizures at me when a deadline is due – sometimes the day before! I tell myself that my health comes first, always. If I were to put everything else before my health, I'd become very unwell.

We have to set boundaries for ourselves and know when we are pushing ourselves too far. I have chronic fatigue so I get tired doing the tiniest tasks, sometimes even just from doing nothing. Writing a book, in all honesty, is draining. I learnt to let myself nap if I needed to, so I could come back to writing with a fresh mind.

No matter how much I'm struggling, though, it helps to know I can lean on my family. My nineteenth birthday came a few months after losing and regaining mobility in my legs. In our household, whenever it's someone's birthday, we all gather in the living room to watch them open their presents.

With both parents and my brothers sat around me smiling, I opened a present and saw that it was a Jacqueline

Wilson book: one of her newer ones which I had never seen before. Do you remember I told you that when I was little I was obsessed with collecting her books? I still loved them, but I was surprised because it had been years since I had received one of her books for my birthday.

I certainly wasn't complaining; I was just confused about why my mum had picked this one. She then told me the book was about a girl named Katy who loses the use of her legs after an accident. This made me smile because now I understood. It made me realise why it's so important to have representation of ourselves in books and to be able to recognise people who look, sound and think like us. It makes you feel seen, and like you're not alone. Knowing that I'm not alone has really helped me get through some of the toughest times in my life.

My worst experience with FND actually happened while I was writing this book. On 12 March 2021, Mum came into my room to start waking me up since it was 11.30am. I was stirring, rolling over and waking up a bit. I rolled on to my back, opened my eyes and just lay there thinking about what I was going to do that day.

Within two minutes, maybe less, I realised I couldn't move. Literally anything. I was paralysed from the neck down. Even my face had been affected, the only thing I could move . . . was my eyes. I couldn't even move my lips. My eyes widened and I started panicking. I couldn't talk so the only thing I could do to get Mum's attention was to make whatever noise I could.

I began groaning loudly. I felt silly but I couldn't do anything else. My mum could tell straight away something wasn't right. She came in and sat with me. I tried to mumble, 'I can't move' and she quickly knew what was going on. She tried to pick me up and hug me because I was getting scared and really upset.

I was crying because it's such a horrible feeling, being fully awake but not being able to move anything. It was like when I couldn't move my legs for the first time in 2018, only much, much worse. Yes, I've been paralysed before but never my whole body.

As she lifted me my head fell backwards and my arms dropped. I couldn't even support my own head. I was like a newborn baby. I couldn't move anything. Not even a finger or a toe.

I think I was in this state for around half an hour, then I gained back some movement in my face, so I could talk now but my jaw was clenched so tight I couldn't open my mouth. Next, I regained movement in my neck; I was able to look around and lift my head. However, everything else was still the same.

Over the next hour, my muscles started locking up. My hands clenched into a fist and my toes and ankles curled – even my butt cheeks were clenched! I was locked up, stiff and I still couldn't lift my arms or legs, so I was still paralysed from the neck down, and I stayed this way for another five hours.

My wonderful mum had to wash my face, change me, do my hair. She put make-up on me to help me feel a bit nicer; she had to brush my teeth for me and feed me. My dad finished work early so he could help out, and him and my mum had to carry me to the toilet. It was so humiliating and it felt like I was paralysed for five days not five hours.

My body eventually relaxed and I was able to join my family at the dinner table that evening. Shortly after dinner, while watching TV with Mum, I had a seizure, which set me right back. When I came out of it my hands had locked up again. It seemed to be slightly less severe this time, as I could still move my arms. I just couldn't unclench my hands. I was gutted that after only just gaining movement back it was taken away again.

So for the rest of the night until I went to sleep I was locked up and shaky again. Luckily when I woke up the following morning I had full mobility but definitely still some seizure activity going on as my eyes were rolling so much.

I had a fairly decent day, despite the annoying tics and eye-rolling. But at around 9pm everything went downhill. I was on the sofa and I began feeling strange, like I was drifting further and further away. This led to a seizure . . . and another one, and another one, and yet another one. I had over five tonic-clonic seizures that night, without coming out of them properly in between.

When the convulsions stopped after roughly the third seizure, I was just totally out of it, looking around the room. I was semi-conscious so I sort of knew what state I was in but I couldn't pull myself round. By this time it was getting late, and Mum suggested we try to get upstairs to bed. I began crying while still being half in a partial seizure. I felt stuck in a seizure state that I couldn't come round from. My mum held me close, which was a huge comfort. My mum and dad got either side of me to help me very slowly walk up the stairs. I remember standing up on wobbly legs, tears rolling off my face and splashing on to the floor. I didn't feel like me at all.

My brain was partially awake but also partially in a seizure. I don't think I can quite find the right words to describe how horrific this feeling is.

I had more seizures once my parents got me into bed. I

had a big long one, then must have fallen straight asleep. I spent the next day recovering.

I am hugely proud of myself. I don't tell myself enough. All of this happened while I was writing this book and had deadlines coming up, so I am thrilled with myself that I managed to still get it all done on time. Sorry, Evie, I should say it more, but you're pretty awesome.

I don't understand how anyone can think FND is fake. Heartbreakingly, even some doctors don't fully believe it, and I've heard of people having awful experiences with medical professionals. Just because there is no evidence for why it happens, it doesn't mean that what we are experiencing isn't real. Why would we choose to live like this? It's so debilitating and life-changing, I'd much rather be 'normal' again.

# A Helping Hand – No Shame

For the last six years, my life has been the epitome of a rollercoaster – there have been high points, but also some huge bumps, twists, turns and moments where I've plunged into very dark tunnels, not knowing if or when they'd end. What I have to show for those six years are some big learnings around how to look after my mental health and how to bolster myself when the going gets tough. Just in case they're useful for any of you reading, I'll tell you about them here!

As I was struggling so much in my early teens, we realised I couldn't get through it by myself. Sometimes we all need a little bit of help to assist us to the light at the end of the tunnel. This is when I was introduced to therapy and medication.

I've seen films and TV series where people hide from their friends that they go to therapy or take medication for their mental health and they try to keep it secret. If you feel this way, please keep reading.

I had my first therapy session when I was fifteen. I

admit that, at first, I was a little embarrassed, and the thought of it was daunting. It was over the years, as I grew more mature, that I wasn't ashamed, and can now talk openly about it.

If we break our leg, we have a cast put on to support the broken bone, but there's no shame in that. So why is it any different getting support for our brain? If we need to take some tablets to help us too, so what? It's just like taking paracetamol to relieve a headache.

As I spoke about on page 169, I've been taking medication daily for about five years so far to control my anxiety and depression and it's really helped me. I'm not saying that it cured me, because it didn't. As well as medication, I did a lot of other things to help myself, like therapy and opening up to my parents whenever I needed to. Medication can really turn things around, but it's not going to do everything for you. If you want recovery, you have to work for it!

Therapy isn't always an option for everyone. Free health-care isn't available everywhere and in the UK our NHS waiting lists can be long, and the appointments can be expensive if you decide to go private. However, if you can afford it, I believe it's really worth investing in something as important as therapy. Not everyone agrees, but I think the right therapist can totally change your life. Surely that's more important than spending your money on takeaways, make-up, etc.?

Like with medication, you may not find the right thera-pist the first time. It's great if you do, but if not, that's okay! You can keep looking and try someone else. Don't decide whether they're right for you on the first or second session, it can take a little while to build up a trusting connection.

*

Here're some questions you can ask yourself to decide whether a therapist is right for you:

- Do you feel comfortable sitting with them?
- Do you feel a weight off when you leave the session?
- Do you feel listened to?
- Are you able to open up to them?
- Do you feel as though you are in a safe space?
- Are they helping you move forwards?
- Do you feel supported?

You may think a therapist is just a stranger you go and vent to without really knowing them, when, actually, having a connection is so important. If you are feeling the opposite of some of those points, there are a few things you can do. You are never stuck, and there are always other options. If after a while things aren't improving and you just aren't clicking with your therapist or counsellor, don't be afraid to ask for someone else. I know it can be uncomfortable, but it's worth it if it involves your recovery and wellbeing.

If you like them as a person but don't like their counselling methods (as a lot of therapists have different methods) you can talk to them about what you'd like them to do differently and how they could improve your sessions with them. I know you may read that and think, 'No way, that's so awkward!' and trust me I get it – younger me would never have done that. However, if you can, I'd really try to push yourself to do it. Afterwards, you can be so proud of yourself, as to others it may seem like no big deal, but as someone with social anxiety and generalised anxiety, I fully understand how much of an achievement this can be. So if you do this or have ever done this, I'm proud of you!

I haven't always had the best luck with counsellors. In fact, I think I had about five until I found the perfect one for me. My first ever real counsellor didn't actually think anything was wrong with me, so of course I wasn't really having the right treatment. After that I tried many more over the years; some I didn't mind, but the methods and type of therapy just weren't working for me. When I was fifteen, I was even put in group therapy to try to manage my social anxiety! I know, I was baffled too! I'm sure they had good intentions, but I didn't cope well with this at all.

When I was nineteen, I was beginning to feel fed up. The therapy I had tried wasn't working for me, but I still needed help. My mum found me a new private therapist, which we had never tried before.

The very first session with a new therapist is always nerve-racking. I wasn't well at all the day I met her so I didn't really take it all in. On the drive to her home I was slightly nervous but mostly I was numb, just staring with no expression. We knocked at her door and she answered with a friendly greeting and a smile.

Regardless of those nerves, after a session or two I quickly realised I quite liked her, and I came away from our hour together feeling better than when I went in. Her name was Liz, and she had a very kind and gentle manner, and was genuinely interested and cared about what I told her. She had a lovely home, which made a calm environment for our sessions, and she always had a candle lit in the room we sat in together.

When I first started with Liz, I had trauma (the one I mentioned earlier, that I'm unable to talk about) which I had tried to work through with other therapists but I just didn't click with them, and when you're being vulnerable enough to talk about trauma, feeling comfortable with them is essential. But with Liz it came so easy. I told her everything and we worked through it bit by bit. We even formed a friendship; she gave me birthday gifts and I made her a mandala canvas for hers.

Liz isn't like any other therapist I've had over the years. She diagnosed me with PTSD – post-traumatic stress disorder – as when I came to her I had been struggling a lot with flashbacks and certain situations. The way she helped me overcome that was amazing, I haven't had a flashback for months. We worked through it together bit by bit, and although it was extraordinarily difficult and uncomfortable at times, it was so worth it.

She also drew up a sheet for us to review at the start of every session, just to check in and see how my week had been. But she had taken the time to customise it; it wasn't just a generic sheet for anyone, it had my personal struggles on. I really appreciated this.

Another thing which really made this therapy work for me was that it didn't just feel all about me. Obviously if you're having therapy you're going to chatter a lot about yourself and that's fine, but Liz told me some of her stories, and this really made me feel as if I knew about her as well as her knowing a lot about me. This isn't for everyone; I know a lot of people may think, 'I'm here for me, not to hear about your life!' which I totally understand! However, Liz did it in a way that I really didn't mind listening to her experience and her side of things.

She also gave her opinion. This was such an important thing for me, as in previous therapy sessions I had told them what I was struggling with and they would say, 'Yeah, yeah, okay', but Liz would tell me what she thought about it and ask me further questions because she was actually interested.

I don't know if Liz realised how much she helped me, but I know she is going to read this book, so I just want to say a massive thank-you. I made more progress with you than any therapist I've ever had since I was fifteen. As you know, I achieved so many of our goals. And I've never done that before. Thank you so much for listening to me, allowing me to talk about such difficult things but making me feel comfortable, and really caring about me – you were a huge factor in my recovery. My whole perspective has changed and, although I did some of the work, you played a huge role!

Also Liz, how cool is this? Some of the things we talked about are in a book! Never saw that coming.

# Support in a Strange Place

Sometimes we find something that helps us in the unlikeliest of places.

Remember when I said I'd joined the Musical.ly app in 2016? My first 'viral' video was in 2018 when it was still Musical.ly, and it was when my FND had just developed. My legs were paralysed and I posted a video of me beginning to be able to walk again after almost a month. It was just a clip of me hobbling along my kitchen but the video received over 3 million views. I was overwhelmed since none of my videos had ever been seen by so many people. Of course, the more views you get, the more idiots will see your video too. So there was the odd comment saying, 'Just walk normally, it's not hard', which is quite funny! But most of the comments were awesome to read through, people saying they were so happy and proud of me.

That support from strangers – knowing that people were willing me on when they'd never even met me – made me feel so warm inside and positive about the world in general.

It shows why we should all be kind to each other because we have extraordinary powers to lift each other up.

My account quickly grew from 20k followers to 100k in less than a week! I was so happy because it meant all those people were now aware of FND, which is what I was aiming for. While it was Musical.ly, it was harder than it is now to have a 'viral' video, so this felt like such a big deal at the time. I was so excited that FND was becoming more well-known because of my video.

An obvious upside of social media for me is of course spreading awareness. From the very beginning, I wanted to talk about what made me who I am. I am a very open person, and so if something was wrong with my health, or my seizures were going through a bad patch, I would talk about it. For me this felt healthy; it was nice to have this weight off my shoulders, and share my struggles with other people. In the beginning I was worried people would think I was attention-seeking, and that's the last thing I'd want. I've never done this for sympathy; it really was to open up people's eyes to what it's like living with disabilities. I was hoping that since people accepted me and my disabilities, they would be more accepting and understanding if they saw another person with something that made them unique.

After that day, I continued posting videos of my FND flare-ups, hoping it would bring more knowledge to this quite unknown condition, as well as keeping up the sign language along to music. I had so many lovely comments on those videos, and over time my sign language improved. When I re-watch my old videos, I sometimes don't even understand what I was trying to sign! It's great to see how much I have grown.

As my account grew, I started opening up about my

seizures, and posting videos of mandalas I had drawn, and talking a little about my tics, even when they were mild.

It was a safe space to vent about my seizures, and my followers were always so lovely. I had roughly 300,000 when Musical.ly transitioned over to TikTok. I didn't mind the change, but it was very different and took a while to get used to.

Followers who watched my videos and enjoyed what I did started asking that I create a YouTube channel. I was a bit daunted by this idea at first because it almost feels like you put yourself out there more if you post videos to YouTube because literally anyone can watch. Eventually I gave in and set up a channel called This Trippy Hippie. I started making videos, some with Peter, some were time-lapses showing the process of drawing a mandala. I used to hate filming YouTube videos by myself. If I was with Peter or a friend it was okay, but by myself, in front of a camera, talking, I hated it. I felt so uncomfortable. I cringed at myself constantly. I'd often build up the courage to just post it, then down the line I'd delete it.

As my confidence grew, I was able to make videos by myself. Now, I can sit talking to a camera for thousands of people to see. I now have a channel full of great Tourette's content – some videos are more light-hearted, like trying tongue-twisters with TS, or baking with TS is always a hoot!

I've had a few ignorant comments regarding this before, and some people think that because I'm making jokes and having fun with my condition, it means I'm doing it for attention. What they don't realise is that living with this every day is really draining. It has an effect on our mental health and it does bring us down sometimes. So if we want to make our Tourette's into something funny and have a laugh about the things that come out of our mouths, we have a right to do that. If we don't laugh, we'll cry!

Social media has many pros but, no matter what type of videos or content you put out there, trolls will always find something to pick on. People are never satisfied, and sometimes just enjoy sitting behind a screen and bringing someone else down. In fact, they're not sitting behind a screen, they're hiding. If you think about it, they would never say any of it to your face, they're just cowards.

The ratio of negative comments to positive ones on my page is basically nothing, but I've still had some pretty nasty ones. A lot of the time it's from people who are lucky enough not to know about Tourette's and who don't understand why I say such things and why I might move in a funny way. So they leave comments like 'She's faking' and 'She's possessed by a demon'. (I know, right!)

When living with a visible disability, unfortunately this makes you an easy target. Another saddo commented and said, 'I hope she never has children so they don't turn out to be a freak like she is.' I can tell you now that if my child has Tourette's, I'm going to be the best mum and I'll be so proud of them. We won't be 'freaks', we'll be stronger than the person who made that comment will probably ever be. A child with TS can feel isolated and scared, wondering what's happening to them. So, if my child does develop tics, I'll be able to understand more than anyone.

Someone told me, 'I'd kill myself if I lived like this.' To be honest, I felt sorry for them. It's a good job I'm made of strong stuff then, and can handle these disabilities like a trouper! Because I do, I know I do.

If you have ever received comments like this, please remember your worth. They make the mistake of thinking we are weak just because we have a disability. Joke's on them!

The vast majority of my audience and followers are so, so lovely, and insanely supportive. My comment sections are always filled with loving messages and words of encouragement, which makes being on social media truly worthwhile. It's a place where you can find encouragement and connection and that has helped me no end.

(Having said that, if you are young and online, please be aware. Don't set up any social media accounts without telling someone, and if something doesn't feel right, it probably isn't. Our gut instincts are usually right, so if something or someone online is making you uncomfortable, talk to your parents or someone you trust about it and they can help you. You can also talk to your school about online safety, because it really is so important. Stay safe out there!)

My profile has led me to connect and make friends with people all over the world, which has been amazing. I met a girl named Nyah who lived in America, and we connected because we both did sign language videos. She was of course doing ASL, but we were so similar in other ways. She was really sweet and was so pretty, but the thing that connected us most was our struggles in the past. She too had lost the use of her legs, and I just couldn't believe it. I had never met anyone like me before, so our friendship felt so special. We both knew what it was like to have such drastic physical symptoms but have no medical explanation.

We'd never met in real life but we became great friends. After months and months of just connecting online, she took a trip to England in July 2018. So at last, we met. We had the biggest hug at the train station, and my family and I showed her around our home town.

Then she came to our house and we made sign language videos together in my bedroom. It was so interesting to compare the differences in the two languages. As expected, we got on really well; I was so smiley all day. A few months later, she came to England again and we had the most wonderful day out together. I was in my wheelchair at the time with paralysed legs, and Nyah pushed me around. She could fully understand because she had been in my position before. We had our nails done together and this was the first time I had ever had a manicure, and I loved it! I felt so girly and grown-up. It was summer so the weather was lovely and warm; we bought ice creams, we went into a beautiful hippie shop and bought matching bracelets to remember this day. It was my favourite out of the two days we spent together.

Nyah is now living her dream life in Hawaii, by the ocean where she feels most at home. I am so happy for her and I'm very proud.

Nyah isn't the only incredible person I've met on TikTok. In 2020, only a few months into the coronavirus pandemic, I posted a video of me baking brownies with my Tourette's causing trouble! I saw a comment from someone who said, 'Evie, when corona goes away we should bake together!' I was curious as to who had said this, and when I looked on her profile, it was a lovely girl called Nikki Lilly. It didn't take me long to see how incredible she was.

Nikki Lilly lives with a condition called Arteriovenous Malformation (AVM) This is when the blood vessels in a certain part of the body don't form correctly, causing the veins to enlarge which leads to swelling, pain and bleeding. Unfortunately, this caused her face to change physically, but she has such an amazing spirit. I had actually seen her before; I knew that she'd been on a TV show called Junior Bake Off when she was only young.

I replied to her comment saying, 'That would be amazing!' and from there we began chatting. We told each other about ourselves and even found out we had exactly the same birthday! We could relate to each other in ways most friends couldn't. We both lived with a life-changing disability and knew what it was like being in hospitals a lot. Nikki Lilly especially has been in hospitals all her life and had countless operations to make her condition more bearable for her. I really admire her. Through everything she remains her sweet, bubbly self and I couldn't be more proud of her.

We added each other on Snapchat and started sending super-long videos to one another. We sent such long videos so that we could really talk about what was going on. So, although we don't talk every day, whenever we have a spare half an hour or so, we listen to all the videos the other person has sent, take it all in and reply with another long video for them to open again later. We've even become pen pals – we write handwritten letters with gifts inside – and we send thoughtful Christmas presents to each other.

These conversations make us feel really close. She is such an amazing friend now; we are hoping that when the Covid-19 situation gets better, we might even get to meet for the first time and celebrate our birthday together!! That would be such a dream. She is always there for me the same way she knows I am always here for her.

Then, in November 2020, I was contacted by two boys called Max and Harvey. I thought the names looked familiar but I couldn't quite put my finger on it. They had messaged me asking me if I would like to be a guest on their podcast. That was when I realised: they are great musicians and came second on a UK TV show called The X Factor: Celebrity in 2019 and are also presenters on CBBC, which is a popular British children's TV channel. I checked out their social media, and even had a quick google which seems so weird now!

I, of course, said I would be honoured. So just before Christmas we recorded the podcast. Unfortunately it had to be recorded online, since because of Covid-19 I couldn't travel to the studio.

It makes me laugh thinking about the moment I was waiting for the meeting to start. I sat in the living room with an iPad in front of me and my anxiety was building up and I even thought about messaging them saying I couldn't do it! I am so glad that I just got on with it because it led to such an amazing friendship.

It was so lovely to meet them and they seemed like such great characters. We chatted about school life, and living with TS, which is one of the main reasons I accepted their invitation, because I'd do anything if it raised awareness of my condition.

After the podcast came out, we started talking regularly, and I got to know them more than I had when doing the recording with them. You realise straight away how fun they are to be around. We are now really great friends, and have been doing live streams together online which everyone seems to be loving so much! Max and Harvey are both equally so supportive of me; right away they accepted me as I am and are always cheering me on. I'm so happy to have got to know them!

To my astonishment, I met the boys in person for the first time in April 2021. I had no clue they were coming – they had planned it with my mum behind my back! The surprise was overwhelming, I was speechless. Me and Mum were on a walk with Teddy when suddenly their loud voices echoed behind us. I knew those voices straight away.

We had a fantastic weekend together, filming videos, taking pictures and just hanging out. Both the boys were amazing with me and my Tourette's, as I knew they would be. That weekend brought us even closer and I'm pretty sure they are friends for life now.

I've also met so many people all around the world who, like me, are living with Tourette's syndrome. We are like a little family now. Some of us are in a group chat where we talk about our days, and if someone is struggling with their tics or other issues, we all come together to support each other. Nothing really compares to having support like that – I'm so grateful to have met such an amazing community of people.

When my tics started getting more severe after having been mild for many years, I felt isolated and like I was going through it alone. I knew I had the endless support of my family, but none of them have tics or TS so they don't fully comprehend what it's like. So when I started showing my tics online, I found all these other people living with the same condition as me, and it was incredible. I no longer felt as if I was going through this alone, I felt understood.

So, to my little group, you know who you are, keep on going and keep your heads up high. I love you!

Social media has many downsides, but it's also an awesome tool to really build a support network. If you haven't found yours yet, it's waiting for you – keep looking!

# Escape into Art

Social media also gave me a really great place to get creative. Some people do that in the form of make-up looks, making music, painting, drawing, anything! Personally, I love sharing photos and videos of my crystals, nature, all things hippie – and my animals. I love showing them off so much that I even set up an account for them, so I can separate it from my main videos about Tourette's and other things. (It's called @animalhipppie if you need something to cheer you up. I'm a very typical animal owner/lover; whenever they do something slightly cute, it's quick: get the camera out and start recording!)

I also enjoy showing people the art I'm working on, especially the pieces I'm proud of! It's great to hear opinions and get feedback. Remember when I said I started drawing mandalas when I was fourteen? Well, I never stopped. One Christmas, Grandma Maggie got me a really pretty notebook. It had a lacey cream cover and plain pages inside. I really loved it and decided to make it my book of mandalas.

The first ever proper 'mandala' I drew was in a pub on Boxing Day. I say 'mandala' in inverted commas because when I first started, they weren't anything special. Every

Boxing Day, it's our family tradition that all of us, including all the grandparents, go to a pub/restaurant for a meal. I took my new notebook and fineliners in my bag with me so I could draw while we waited for our food to arrive. I traced a circle around the bottom of one of the glasses and began adding different patterns and details. I remember feeling so proud of it, but when I look at it now it's so wobbly!

I took this notebook everywhere with me. I brought it to hospital with me when I was unwell, and it went with me to college every day. Every spare minute I had at college I was drawing a mandala in my notebook. While being mute, drawing mandalas was an escape for me. I couldn't speak to people so I just kept my head down in my notebook and kept drawing. If you're going through a tough time, I would really recommend finding a creative outlet to focus on – it doesn't matter how good you are, it's like an icepack for your brain!

Yet, perhaps unsurprisingly given that 'practice makes perfect' saying, over the months and years my mandalas have massively improved. The designs got bigger, the patterns were more intricate and the lines were straighter. In the last year or so, I've even had people think I'm filling in a colouring sheet – they don't realise I've drawn all of it, which is a huge compliment!

In 2019, after showing my mandalas online for so long and with my following growing, people were saying that they would buy my mandalas if I sold them. I felt so humbled, so I tried setting up an Etsy shop. This process took a while, figuring out payment methods and postage. I wasn't very good at it in the beginning; I'd never done anything like this before. I of course named my shop 'This Trippy Hippie' so people could find me easily.

I built up a big art stock and put around twelve items up

for sale, like decorated wooden boxes, canvases and photo frames with my mandalas inside. I announced online about my new shop and everything sold out in fifteen or twenty minutes! For my first sale, this was amazing. I was so proud of myself that my mandalas and designs were now at a level where I was able to sell them around the world and people actually wanted to buy them. I no longer looked online for mandala inspiration, I could make my own original designs.

I don't sell on Etsy too regularly, because mandalas can take hours and hours and it takes a while to build up stock again. Especially when I'm doing other incredible things like writing a book! These days, whenever I have a restock on my shop, I'm not exaggerating when I say it all sells out in sometimes less than a minute. This is so incredible, but I know it can be frustrating for the people who wanted to buy something but just missed out.

People often tell me that they wouldn't have the patience to draw mandalas, which I fully understand! It does take a lot of patience. I've had people also tell me that my designs would make great tattoos. As I mentioned earlier, if it wasn't for my heart defect, I would without a doubt have one of my mandalas tattooed on my arm. But just because I had to miss out, didn't mean everyone else did! Peter was getting a new tattoo, and he asked me to design a mandala for him. I was honoured that he wanted one of my designs on his skin for ever, and I designed him a yin-yang mandala. He loved it and later on had it tattooed on his calf. It was an amazing feeling to see my art on someone's skin.

To anyone reading this who has bought my art, or anything from my shop, I want to say a massive thank-you. It really is a huge confidence boost to know that, out there, people have my art hanging up in their homes. I really believe in making your bedroom your safe space, so if my art can bring someone's room to life a bit more, I have succeeded in my mission.

A lot of people ask me, 'How can you draw mandalas with Tourette's?' I understand: if my Tourette's causes me to jerk around and have no control over my body, surely I'd mess up and just scribble all over the paper? Well, even before my tics were severe, drawing mandalas always had a huge calming effect. When I developed severe Tourette's, it was no different. As soon as my pen touches the paper and I begin drawing, my TS kind of 'disappears' and the tics reduce massively. I still have little head twitches, facial tics and some sounds, but nothing that would affect my drawing too much. However, if I was having a full-on tic attack, I wouldn't let myself anywhere near my mandalas. My tic attacks are far too strong – even drawing mandalas wouldn't calm me down.

Most individuals with Tourette's have an activity that makes their TS 'go away'. For some it's playing music, singing, a sport, art, any hobby that requires their full attention. Being focused uses a different part of the brain to the one where scientists believe the signals are misfiring, causing the tics. So when we focus on something, we don't tic as much. The brain is so fascinating, and, like the ocean, there's so much of it we still don't know.

On the following pages you'll find a couple of mandalas I designed specially for this book. Unwind and colour them however you like. Don't worry too much about being neat or perfect, just enjoy doing it!

# My Four-Legged Friends

Therapy, community and art have all helped me to find strength when things have been difficult. But – as I might have said before! – something else that has been invaluable to me has been my animals.

I've mentioned that we have a dog called Teddy. He came into our lives in October 2018. My mum called me into her room one dark evening and she showed me a picture of puppies and said, 'What do you think?'

I smirked, thinking she was tricking me. I asked her what she meant and she told me that a friend of a friend's dog had given birth to a beautiful litter of puppies. She said, 'Now we just have to convince Dad!' and that's when I knew she was serious. I couldn't believe what I was hearing. I had wanted a dog since I was a little girl and we had never had one because, during the weekdays, everyone was out at school or work.

But at this point, Mum had recently quit her job to become a full-time carer to me after my mental health and seizures hit rock bottom. So now someone was going to be in the house! We showed Dad the photos and obviously his first reaction was, 'No, absolutely not!' He was worried about the financial implications and believed we already had enough animals.

But, after some convincing, Dad agreed! Mum arranged with the lady for us to go and see the puppies and even to pick one out. I felt so excited on that car ride I could have peed myself.

The lady was so lovely; we all walked upstairs and waited in a bedroom. A couple of minutes later, the door opened, and around six or seven tiny little puppies with short stumpy legs came trotting through and came straight over to us. I was immediately laughing at how funny they all looked running towards us!

I was totally in my element, and because we'd never owned a dog I'd never really been around puppies like this before. I was stuck with a constant smile on my face the whole time we were there. They were all so cheeky; some were more shy than others, but a lot of them were interested in my backpack. It was on the floor next to me and at least three of the puppies chewed on some keyrings and climbed all over it!

They all had similar colouring; some were darker, almost a black colour, but two of them were charcoal grey, with cream coming through underneath. Mum sat with one of the puppies cuddled into her almost the whole time. He was one of the ones with the different fur and was wearing a tiny blue Velcro collar.

Dad and I sat on the floor with all the others. As well as the one Mum was holding, I really liked one of the girls – I thought she was quite sweet. She was a little bit more timid, but she was licking my hands and seeming quite cuddly.

When we returned home, we had a decision to make. In the end we decided on the boy. The girl was so sweet and gentle, but we loved the cheeky boy's fur, and we were intrigued as to what his coat would look like as he grew. I remember we were sitting on the sofa that evening discussing names. We thought Teddy would be perfect because of his fluffy appearance and toy-like face.

We had a little while to prepare to bring him home, so I did lots of research, and we did a big puppy shop. This was such an exciting day, I made a video about it on my YouTube! I pretty much emptied my wallet buying so many things for him – one of them being a stuffed toy monkey, which at the time was actually twice the size of him!

On 27 October 2018, we went to bring home our new family member. The lady cried a little as we took him to the car. Teddy's original name was Albert, named after the lady's dad. So Teddy's full name is Teddy Albert – we wanted to keep it since it was so special to her.

We wrapped him up in his brand-new puppy blanket and I carried him to the car with me and sat with him on my knee. Poor little Teddy was shaking during the journey so I cuddled him to make him feel safe. I was beaming the whole way home.

Teddy was a spoilt dog from the day he came home. His first week with us was filled with belly massages, treats, and many cuddles. I was obsessed with him. My head was filled with puppy thoughts and he made me feel so much better.

If I had to leave him to go to college, I spent the whole day looking forward to seeing him when I got home. It took him a little while to gain confidence in his new home and get used to being away from his mum and siblings, but we soon saw his character coming through.

Like most dogs, he loves playing with a ball and zooming around. When we first got him, being next to a tennis ball made him look as if he had shrunk in the wash but he liked nudging it around anyway. As Teddy went through his 'toddler' stage, we saw his fur begin to change, just as Mum had predicted. As his fur grew longer, he lost his deep grey and started turning a cream colour. Before long, he looked like a totally different dog to the dark-coloured puppy we brought home that day!

Just like having a new baby, we went through all the puppy milestones! His first walk, his first wee outside, his first Christmas, learning his first trick, all those lovely things that make a puppy mummy very proud!

Although Dad had been fully against having a dog for years, it didn't take long for him to be totally smitten with Teddy. Soon he was taking selfies with him, napping with him, kissing him all over, etc., etc. (He won't like me saying that!)

I have too many memories of Teddy as a youngster to put into this book – so many, in fact, that they could have their own book! But one of my favourites was when he was only seven months old.

Mum and I walked him over the field at the back of our house, and went to a dog-friendly pub for a nice lunch together. For some reason, when Teddy is on a large open patch of grass he goes crazy, so he started zooming around, spinning my mum in circles as she held the lead. His eyes were so wide!

When we got to the pub, we ordered our food and Teddy sat on the floor in between our chairs. But he wouldn't stay still and kept walking around so the lead was getting tangled up round the chair and table legs. Because of this, Mum and I discussed whether he'd be okay if we let him off the lead, thinking he would just sit with us if we did so. So I detached the lead from his collar.

Within a couple of minutes Teddy jumped up and zoomed off, running like a lunatic under people's tables as they were trying to eat their meals. My mum jumped up and ran after him, calling his name and apologising to the families who were just trying to enjoy their food!

I probably should have helped a bit more but I was just laughing hopelessly. Eventually Mum caught a hold of him and dragged him back over to our table. She sighed and said, 'For goodness sake, Teddy, that was embarrassing.' I laughed so much my cheeks hurt. He made a bit of a fool out of us that day but I think it made me love him even more!

When we were thinking about getting a dog, we hoped that whoever it was could somehow help during one of my seizures. We were hoping to train them to maybe bark when I was seizing to get attention, in case I wasn't with anyone. We had heard of dogs alerting to seizures before and it just seemed amazing, so from Teddy being only a couple of months or so old, we made him aware of my seizures, and Mum would bring him to me so he could be with me and watch me having them.

When he was tiny, he wasn't really that bothered! As he grew older and matured a bit more, I think he started to realise that something wasn't quite right and could recognise that when I had one. Now when I have a seizure, Teddy knows what's going on. He often sits with me and licks my hands. I've seen a few videos of what he's like with me during a seizure; sometimes my mum will film him to show me.

One video I saw is really sweet – my arms are convulsing and he tries to give me his paw. He also recognises if my breathing isn't normal. He sometimes tilts his head as he listens carefully to the sound of my breathing.

Teddy has never been properly trained to help me when I do have seizures, I think mostly because I always have someone near me like my mum. Just having him close by when I come round from the seizure is comforting enough. Mum sometimes takes my hand when I'm seizing and uses it to stroke Teddy, to ground me and help me feel something familiar.

When my tics got worse, Teddy quickly adjusted to the new sounds I made. He barely pays any attention now; he just knows it's something I do! During a tic attack, he worries a little less I think because he can see that I'm still me. I can still communicate and I'm still conscious and I think he knows that.

When I am in a tic attack I am full of energy, and sometimes Teddy likes to join in and he starts jumping around! This isn't massively helpful, bless him, but he thinks I'm playing. I also get 'Tourette's zoomies' as Mum and I like to call them, which is when my tics make me run around the house with that energy feeling going up and down my legs. Teddy thinks this game is hilarious!

Teddy doesn't only help my physical problems, though. Teddy arrived during one of the roughest mental health patches I have ever been through. Depression is an awful illness and can make you feel unlovable, worthless, like you're nothing, but coming home and seeing how happy Teddy was to see me just turned those feelings around. His bum starts wriggling, his tail is wagging and he gets his 'happy feet', when he energetically pats his feet on the floor, and it made me feel so loved.

I no longer feel worthless or unlovable at all, but even now when I come through the door and Teddy runs over to see me, I still feel so loved. Knowing that you make an animal that happy, and seeing how much you mean to them, it's an amazing feeling.

Teddy's seen a few animals come and go in his time. After we said goodbye to Beano, I used to wonder if Teddy ever wondered where he had gone. And my rabbits Lola and Pip also died after getting that terrible bunny virus. My mum said that when I was ready, I could try having bunnies again – she knew that rabbits were a special animal to me.

In late 2019, I therefore rescued two English Spot rabbits. Brothers, which I named Wilbur and Georgie (with the help of Mum!). It felt really nice to rescue them rather than buy them from a pet shop. And, once again, my rabbit care and knowledge had improved. I was glad to get them out of that rescue home, since I wasn't very impressed with the conditions and environment.

When I brought the boys home, Wilbur had bloodstains on him, and still had a metal ring round his back leg. The man at the rescue place told us Wilbur and Georgie were going to be show rabbits, but since their markings and spots weren't 'identical enough' they had been dumped there. It makes me sad thinking about what they must have gone through so I was really looking forward to giving them a new life!

Within a few hours of being home, we realised they had to be separated. They were fighting, but not just little scraps, really violent fights. It was scary to watch, and we had to keep them apart so they didn't get severely injured. We then realised that maybe the blood on Wilbur was from the fighting, but the rescue home hadn't realised so they had been kept together.

So we made separate enclosures and sadly the boys couldn't go back together. I tried giving them bonding sessions but they just really disliked each other! Sibling rivalry! So I got to know their personalities individually.

Georgie was a really lovely bunny with such a nice nature. He was black and white, whereas Wilbur was grey and white. English Spot rabbits have such impressive markings, so I've always admired them. The classic English Spot marking is the striking stripe that goes right down their back, usually surrounded by spots.

Georgie was very outgoing; he liked having people around and Teddy liked him too! Often if Teddy went up to the rabbit run, Georgie would hop over and let Teddy give him a little lick.

Wilbur wasn't as outgoing; he could be very shy and liked his own company. He still loved being fed yummy greens, but I found it easier to connect with Georgie because of his nature. I had to work with Wilbur to build up his confidence a bit.

Only two months down the line, my bad luck with rabbits struck again. It turned out Georgie had been sick since he'd been at the rescue home, and had many underlying health conditions, one of them being that his eye was so badly damaged he couldn't even open it anymore. He went to the vet's for an operation close to Christmas but sadly didn't make it past the blood test.

During all of this, I had the most amazing veterinarian. It was a lady who specialised in small animals, and she knew exactly what she was talking about. The thing that made her special was that she really cared about Georgie. Vets do care, of course, but they see so many animals a week that some of them can't build a connection. However, this lady really liked Georgie; she was extra gentle with his tiny body and always chose the best options for him. She was with him when he passed away and I'm glad it was her. I wrote her a card afterwards thanking her for how amazing she was with him. I'll always be grateful.

I had a real soft spot for Georgie. While caring for a sick animal you can get really attached, which makes saying goodbye harder. I'm proud of the way I looked after him; I did everything right.

And I'm proud that this time I knew how to deal with the loss of Georgie in a way that let me grieve, but didn't negatively impact my mental health. Therapy, medication, community and doing my mandalas had created a sort of cotton-wool padding around my brain, so that even though I was really sad, I could deal with what was happening much better. I think it's so important to build up methods of dealing with dark times because of course they do happen to all of us at some point. The day after little Georgie's passing, Mum went into the dining room for a while and I was in my room drawing. Later she came upstairs with the sweetest drawing for me. She had drawn Georgie.

She said, 'I drew him with his eye better, so you can remember him as before he was poorly.' I cried looking at the picture – she'd captured his lovely face perfectly. I hugged her so tight; this gesture was so much appreciated.

Now Wilbur was on his own, and although he'd been living separately from Georgie, I'd put their enclosures right next to each other so they could say hello through the bars. I knew that rabbits can get lonely on their own, and can even develop depression, so I wanted to get him a friend. I was determined to have some good luck with my rabbits! So, coming into the New Year, I began looking for another bunny. Only a week into January, I brought home an eleven-week-old French Lop, which I named Bonnie. I have loved the name Bonnie for years, especially after watching *Toy Story 3*! French Lop is the sixth largest breed of rabbit in the world, so Bonnie was already big for her age. It was an amazing way to start 2020.

Although I've owned six rabbits so far, Bonnie has the strongest personality out of them all. She's not afraid to tell you what she wants – she comes with lots of sound effects! I've never had a bunny be so noisy. She has a sound for every emotion! If she's happy and really loving what she's eating, she makes loud contented grunting noises. If you touch her when she doesn't want you to, for example when she's eating, she lets out a sharp angry grunt. If you take too long to feed her, she stomps her humongous back feet, which makes such a racket!

Very quickly, Bonnie grew bigger and bigger and bigger!

By the time she was around ten months old, she was the same size as our lovely cat Lottie, with ridiculously huge back feet! But she has such a sweet girly face, with round cheeks and dark eyes with long black eyelashes. Her fur is heavenly soft.

I did try bonding her with Wilbur of course, as that was the plan when I bought her. However, we came to the conclusion that Wilbur just doesn't like other rabbits. He liked being with me, but other rabbits were a no-go. I didn't like stressing them both out and didn't want any more injuries, so they've remained separate since, but I think they are still very happy.

When Bonnie was roughly five months old, I invested in a big rabbit shed for her. I knew she was only going to continue to get bigger and chunkier, so keeping her in a hutch with a run attached wasn't an option. So now, my spoilt bunny has her own home! It has sheltered areas, levels for her to climb which she loves, and blankets to snuggle in.

I really love having two rabbits that are totally different. Bonnie and Wilbur look like total opposites, not only because of their appearance, but because their characters are so different too.

Bonnie has an attitude, loves to get her own way, but is still very, very friendly, and she's not shy in the slightest! She will happily hop over to see a stranger and greet them. Her all-time favourite foods are grapes, banana, parsley and her rabbit nuggets. Did you know that if a bunny is really enjoying their food they twitch their bums? Bonnie never does anything half-heartedly, so when she's enjoying a piece of fruit, her butt twitches so dramatically it looks like she's twerking!

The thing I adore most about Wilbur is his love of sun-bathing. Most rabbits do love sitting in the sun, but Wilbur loves it more than anything, even more than food. Wilbur's breed is very thin and dainty, with not very thick fur, which I think is a reason he loves the warmth so much. He can sit in the sun for hours and not get too hot. He finds a lovely bit of sun in his run, gets comfy, does the 'loaf', which is a common rabbit position, and puts his ears back to relax. He gently closes his eyes and just sits there soaking up the sun and getting some vitamin D! I just adore it when he does this.

Whenever we have a sunny day, I love to let the bunnies run around the garden. They have to do this one after the other, but any day when the rabbits are out is a day of me being in a good mood!

Wilbur loves it; he's often a bit reluctant to get back in his hutch! Bonnie shows her love of being in the garden a different way – binkies and zoomies! If you are unfamiliar with the bunny terminology, a 'binky' is when a rabbit suddenly jumps into the air while twisting their body and flicking their head. A binky is an expression of pure joy and happiness! So, when I see Bonnie or Wilbur do this, it immediately makes me and anyone watching smile. Especially when it's Bonnie – she doesn't hold back!

My two bunnies (as well as Teddy, Lottie and my fish!) are still happily living with me, and are very well cared for and extremely loved. I'm hoping I'll have them for many more years; I don't want to lose them. They are my Tourette's and anxiety 'cure'!

When I'm around Bonnie or Wilbur, my tics significantly decrease. The violent ones calm down and I feel myself relax. Even better, when I hold them, it all just goes away. Especially Wilbur. As much as I love my big chunky girl, Bonnie is very wriggly! I love stroking her soft fur, but she is too adventurous to just sit with me. Wilbur on the other hand will sit calmly with me. As soon as he is in my arms, I can just feel my Tourette's go away for a while. I still have the odd eye-roll or facial tic, but my body doesn't jerk or shout.

He is such a good boy, I wish he knew how much he's helped me. Wilbur calms my Tourette's more than any of my other animals. He's so special.

Animals don't just help people with Tourette's, they have helped many others with a variety of disabilities, learning and physical. If you are struggling and think animal therapy could really benefit you, I would have a look at your options. Are you well enough to care for something as high maintenance as a dog or a rabbit? If not, maybe a cat would be perfect! They are great for cuddles in bed, and you don't need to take them for walks every day. Or perhaps a small animal, two mice or a couple of guinea pigs; they can still be just as calming. But make sure you don't get a small cage! (Like rabbits, you should always buy guinea pigs in bonded pairs, and mice like the company of each other too – two females are best to avoid unwanted babies or fighting.)

If having a pet is not something that could work for you, don't worry. Why not ask your neighbour or a friend if you could take their dog for a walk? Or, there are many lovely farms out there which allow you to feed lambs, hold the chicks, bunnies and guinea pigs. Animals have done wonders for me and I hope they can do the same for you.

# Finding Myself

It was 2016 when I discovered my style and really found a new part of me. I had seen a girl on YouTube with a bohemian/hippie style and I was immediately drawn to her. I spent hours watching through her videos and thinking how absolutely stunning she was. I looked through my clothes to see if I had anything similar. I didn't have much, but I found a shirt and from there began building a new wardrobe.

As I changed my style of clothes – and started redecorating my room to match – I had new feelings that I hadn't experienced before. I felt a huge sense of belonging and peace.

I know that being at secondary school and exploring your style is difficult. Everyone there wants to look the same to 'fit in', so to look a bit different can be really daunting. We shouldn't have to worry about being judged or even bullied for our appearance, but unfortunately that's the way secondary school has been for years and years. I admit, when I started finding myself, I would change my clothes before I left the house. My clothes and style were different, and there was no one like me around. This scared me a lot; I didn't want to stand out or draw attention to myself.

I love wearing hippie/harem pants, which are loose trousers made with beautiful patterned material, but I hadn't seen anyone else wear them before so in my eyes that made me 'look weird'. So before we left the house I would change into plain black leggings. I don't mind wearing leggings, but I'd rather be in my beautiful hippie pants.

It took quite a long time for me to stop caring about being different. Now I wear whatever I want and I look good while doing it! That's not being big-headed or cocky, it's just self-confidence and self-acceptance.

To be honest, I now feel a little sorry for all the people who look the same as everyone else. Must be so boring!

If you are in secondary school and are struggling with having a 'unique' style, I think you look awesome! It takes guts to stand out from the crowd and, honestly, I think it's an amazing thing. Feel proud of yourself that you have found a way to express yourself and you aren't afraid to do so. Whatever kind of style you choose, just make sure it's really reflecting you and that you've chosen it for yourself. Because I have found so much happiness in feeling like me on the outside that it's supported everything going on in the inside.

It's been years since I discovered my style and I have grown so much. I am my own person with my own individuality and my bedroom is beautiful. Especially during times of struggle with mental health, making your room into your own little haven can really have a positive impact. I may be a little plant crazy but I really do recommend a beautiful vibrant plant for your room. I instantly feel a boost just by looking at mine, and you can research ones that are easy to care for if you're worried about killing it!

Finding your style is such an exciting thing, being unique is so great and nothing to be scared of.

I suppose that part of my style now is my Tourette's, and I actually think it's helped my confidence a lot. It may sound strange, but I've had social anxiety for years – scared of people looking at me, scared of having any attention drawn to myself. I hid away from it as much as I could, not really pushing myself. When my tics got louder and more severe, it was out of my control and it did draw attention to me. Heads would turn, wondering why I was shouting or making strange noises.

So I had no choice. My Tourette's forced me to come out of my shell.

Although I was so uncomfortable at first, I'm grateful for my TS. It helped me work through my social anxiety which I had been trying to do for years.

# I am Lovable!

When you have a disability, you might sometimes think you are unlovable, or that no one will want to be in a relationship with you just because you are different. I'm here to prove otherwise!

When my seizures became more severe and frequent, I felt so ugly I never wanted anyone to look at me when I had one. I thought to myself that no one would like me if they saw me seizing.

Peter and I had been best friends for two years, when eventually, on 9 November 2019, we became a couple. Bless him, he was kept in the friendzone for so long!

I knew about his feelings for me very early on, but because of my trauma and PTSD from a previous relationship, I was too scared. It took two whole years for me to finally be ready to be in a relationship again. During this time Peter had told me that those feelings for me had gone away, so I was incredibly nervous to tell him that I was beginning to fall for him. What if I'd missed my chance?

The evening it happened, I was in my room; it was over the phone because Peter was at home, and I told him how I was feeling. I was so relieved when he told me that the feelings he had for me never went away. I knew he had lied!! He only said that because he knew I wasn't ready and he didn't know if I felt the same. I was so smiley that night!

Peter had waited two years. He had feelings for me for two years and just put up with it because he knew I was healing. He never once pressured me, he just stuck by my side.

Peter is one of those people you rarely come across. Not everyone is lucky enough to have someone like him. Someone who loves you no matter what, someone who accepts you on good and bad days. Someone who has seen you at your worst and thinks no different of you.

In 2018 and 2019, I was in hospital a lot with my seizures being so bad. On multiple occasions, I'd be lying in a hospital bed with a cannula in my arm and feeling so rubbish, when Peter would appear and sit with me and Mum, making me smile and lifting my spirits.

He is also fully accepting of and adjusted to my Tourette's. It's not easy being in a relationship with TS, as my tics make me hit and punch Peter and I really hate it. It can't be easy for him, either, but he knows that it's not me doing it; he reminds me that it's okay every time.

Peter knows that my TS will be with me for life, and he has told me that he's sticking with me through it all. Sorry to be so soppy! I'm just so grateful for him.

Our relationship has really come such a long way. Due to the nature of my trauma, when Peter and I first became friends, I wouldn't allow him to close the door if we were in a room by ourselves. There were days when I wouldn't let him touch me. I was with my therapist Liz at the time and it took us months to work through this.

With her help and Peter's patience and understanding, we can now be in a room together with the door closed. I'll happily cuddle with him anytime and just have a normal healthy relationship! I'm so proud of those achievements.

Feeling loved is one of the warmest emotions. Everyone deserves to feel loved, it's a basic human right. Knowing that someone loves you, regardless of whatever disability you may have, is just amazing.

Peter loves me – Tourette's, seizures, FND, mental health and all, and it's really boosted my confidence. I know that I am worthy of love and that I am lovable! And whoever you are, disability or no, you are lovable too.

# The Reality of Living with a Disability

Individuals reading this who have a disability will know that our everyday routines aren't quite the same as everyone else's.

Here's how my morning usually goes:

- Wake up – the first thing I usually say is 'Beans!' which is my most common tic.
- My Tourette's lets everyone know I'm awake by shouting and swearing.
- Go downstairs for breakfast; I sometimes have to slide down the stairs on my bum if my tics are making me fall over.
- Make breakfast; usually get food everywhere, my tics like to throw things and make a mess.
- Make a drink; usually gets spilled on the floor.
- Take my medication.
- Punch a few walls along the way!

That's just my morning, the rest of the day really depends on what we're doing. If we're having a chill day and I'm mostly in my room, drawing, watching Netflix or whatever, I'm usually fairly calm. If we go down to the shop, that can be interesting. I wear my badge that says 'Tourette's' just so people are aware if I say anything strange. Shopping with Tourette's can be quite a big trigger. I feel so conscious of people looking at me, and I become very aware of my tics. I sometimes shout words, sometimes I just randomly yell, and I might throw something. My Tourette's also has an odd obsession with anyone who is bald. So as soon as I see someone in the shop, I immediately shout, 'Baldy!' So far, thankfully, I've had no issues. It's super-embarrassing, though. I hate it. I never realised how many bald men were out there!

As we leave the shop, or even when we're paying at the till, I'll say, 'We're shoplifting! Thief!' and I have no control over it, it just comes out. We usually start speed-walking after that and get out of the shop as quickly as possible before we get stopped by security!! (Just to clarify, we never actually shoplift!)

Every day at around 6pm, my family and I all sit at the table for dinner. Something as simple as eating dinner can be hard with Tourette's like mine. Like I said, TS is a spectrum and some people with TS will have no issues at all; it depends on the type of tics you have.

I don't drink from glasses anymore, for two reasons. One is that there's always a chance I could smash the glass; the other, which happens often, is that my arms jerk when I'm holding the glass and the juice spills all over me and the table. So instead we found a solution. I now have tall bottles with a lid and a straw inside, which is so much more convenient for me. It means that even if my arms are going all over the place, I don't spill anything.

It's not just drinking that's an issue, though. Sometimes I'll stab food on to my fork, but then my arms jerk violently and the food goes flying off the fork. There've been a few occasions where I've picked the food up with my hands and thrown it across the room, leaving splatter marks on the wall! It sounds naughty, but it's fully involuntary, meaning I don't control it. Even using cutlery can be dangerous on a bad tic day. I have to be careful and my parents monitor me. My tics also make me stab the table with my knife and fork, which means our wooden dining-room table has many, many chips and scratches in it. You can tell straight away where I sit! We have a solution for that too, though – we put cork placemats on either side of my plate, so my tics stab those instead.

Writing this book hasn't always been easy, either. When I am really involved and fully engrossed in a chapter, I don't struggle too much, but if my tics are bad, my hands slam on the keyboard and mess up what I'm typing. Or they punch my laptop. This can be really frustrating for me, when I'm trying to do such an important and incredible thing!

When I feed my rabbits on a night, I change their water bowls, give them some greens, and some nuggets. The water bowls are the hardest. Carrying them inside to the sink is okay, but once I've filled them up, I then have to carry them outside, keeping them as still as possible. When you have Tourette's, 'still' isn't really in your vocabulary. I have a tic where my hands tip and pour out all the water as soon I've filled up the bowls. This gets me really worked up; sometimes I have to refill each bowl three times. If I get too frustrated Mum will do it for me.

As you can imagine, things like getting a haircut or having my nails done aren't a walk in the park either. My hairdresser knows about my disability so she's totally understanding and will pause if my tics are getting too strong. I don't go to the hairdresser if I just need my fringe trimming, though; my mum does that for me. She is very patient! She will have hold of the piece of fringe she's going to cut and my tics will jerk backwards and she has to try again. This happens over and over and over again. Just a simple tiny fringe trim can take twenty minutes.

I don't get my nails done often at all, but I sometimes go for acrylics to make myself feel pretty. At first, when my tics were mild, it wasn't an issue at all. However, when they got more severe, it became difficult. I would have to suppress my tics just so the nail artist could manage to get anything done.

A check-up at the dentist's can be really nerve-racking. I don't like making their jobs harder! They allow me to listen to music through headphones during the appointment, which makes such a big difference. I know that without this it would be very different. They are very understanding and accepting, and don't seem to mind my tics at all. During my check-up my tics sometimes close my mouth when they're trying to look at my teeth! This isn't ideal.

Virtually any task with Tourette's is going to be a little different from the average person, and trying to keep my cool and not get angry is another challenge itself. I often manage this by cuddling with Teddy or putting some music on.

# Answering Your Questions About Living with Tourette's

These are all questions which I have been asked on my social media, so hopefully by answering them you will have a better understanding of Tourette's ...

*'Do you tic in your sleep?'*

This varies for everyone. Most people with TS do not tic in their sleep. On the other hand, some, like me, do. I have twitched in my sleep for years; I have motor tics, such as my hands and arms jerking and my legs jumping. However, I do not shout swear words in my sleep!!

### 'Do you tic 24/7?'

No one with TS tics every second of every day. We can have periods where our tics are more severe, but every individual with Tourette's has something that calms their tics, usually some kind of hobby. For example, when I draw my mandalas I don't tic much at all. For others it may be ice-skating, singing, playing an instrument. We can have days where it feels like our tics are almost constant, but eventually they will settle down again.

### 'How do you know when you're going to have a tic attack?'

Building up to a tic attack, we feel energy running through our veins. For me it almost feels like I've been electrocuted, or as if I have 'ants in my pants'! It's an awful feeling; I have so much energy and my body doesn't know what to do with it – that's when the tics get worse and worse then go into a full-blown tic attack.

### 'Does your Tourette's make you tired a lot?'

As you can imagine, twitching and uncontrollably saying things every day is going to make anyone tired. The thing about Tourette's is, even if we feel tired and can't be bothered to move, our bodies will jerk and twitch anyway. When my tics began getting more active, I was exhausted all the time at first. It's been a while now, and although I have chronic fatigue, my body has adjusted to my tics and copes a lot better.

### 'Do you know what's about to come out of your mouth?'

For most of us, what we say is just as shocking for us as it is for you. Sometimes when I say something hilarious or rude, I'll put my hands over my mouth and think, 'What the heck?!' I often can't believe what I've just said. It's so strange because it feels like someone else is speaking for me and I can't quite keep them inside. This is why I call my Tourette's my nonidentical twin!

### 'Are you possessed?'

Believe it or not, I've been told many times online that I am possessed and need to be freed from the monster inside me. As much as I respect people's beliefs, this makes me feel as if I'm not even human. I am just like you; I just have a slight difference in my brain that causes me to twitch and say things.

### 'Will your tics ever go away?'

Unfortunately, Tourette's syndrome is a lifelong condition. If I had a tic disorder, or childhood tics, then yes, I could have grown out of them. However, because I have Tourette's now, I'm going to have it for the rest of my life. There is still hope, though; this doesn't mean that I'm always going to have it at this severity. Maybe when I'm older my tics will be more mild.

### 'Are you able to drive with Tourette's?'

Many individuals with Tourette's have their driver's licence. It really depends on the person and what particular tics they have. Someone could have a more severe case of TS but still drive because driving might calm them down, or maybe they don't have any tics that interfere with driving.

Yet someone else with a more mild case of Tourette's might not be able to drive because of the types of tics they have. For example, they might have a tic where they close their eyes. Of course while driving this could be very dangerous.

I am unable to drive, but this isn't due to my TS. I can't drive because of my seizures. I've never even been able to take a single lesson.


### 'How did you get your piercings?'

All of my piercings were done before my Tourette's became severe. My newest piercings, like my nose piercings (although they were done years ago) were done when I had tics, but they weren't severe enough for it to have been an issue.


### 'What's the difference between a tic attack and a seizure?'

Tic attacks are fully caused by Tourette's whereas seizures aren't. During a tic attack I am fully conscious and know what's going on; however, for most seizures I am unconscious or semi-conscious. The movements are different too, so during a tic attack, of course I am ticcing. Whereas during a seizure I am convulsing. Hopefully that makes sense!

*'Can you hold in your tics?'*

It is possible to hold in tics for a short period of time. In Tourette's terms, this is called **suppression** (see page 153). Imagine you are in a silent exam hall, and you really need to cough. Sitting in silence, you feel the cough tickling and building up in your throat. This is how it feels to suppress our tics. It can be harmful and can lead to big tic attacks afterwards. So I only suppress if I absolutely have to, for example at the dentist's.

# For My Fellow 'Touretters'

This chapter I want to dedicate to those of you reading this who have Tourette's, a tic disorder or tics caused by anything else such as anxiety.

First of all, I hope this book has brought you some comfort, or at least made you feel less alone. But hey, how are you doing? I hope your tics have been good to you today.

If you have strategies to deal with your tics, and are aware of what helps you, that's great! If you are unsure about how to put things in place, don't worry, I'm here to help! I'm going to talk about things we have put in place for my particular tics, and maybe you'll find it helpful. These won't apply to everyone; some of you might not have any issues with these things. It all depends on the type of tic you're struggling with, but hopefully I can give you some ideas.

I understand that for some of us, mealtimes can be tricky. If you struggle with drinking, and drinks being spilled, etc., I really recommend purchasing an adapted water bottle. You can get them from any supermarket really; they are tall with a screw-on lid that has a straw attached and a sippy part that can usually be folded down. I use them every time I want a drink now. It's such a relief – I don't have to worry about suppressing my tics just to have a drink.

If using a knife and fork is too dangerous, you could try plastic cutlery. I know it may feel babyish and a little embarrassing, but I think it feels better than hurting yourself!

Tic attacks can be painful and harmful. Especially if you have nothing in place to help. Depending on the tics that occur for you during an attack, a crash helmet may be helpful. I have had black eyes from my Tourette's and many big blows to the head. So I bought myself a crash helmet, the sort usually used in boxing matches. And let me tell you it does the job perfectly! It completely softens the blow and can fully prevent too much damage.

Protective gloves are something else I have found that work great. Tourette's often makes us flail our arms and hands about and sometimes punch things. Our hands can get sore and beaten, so if you have tics that injure your hands, looking into getting some protective gloves can be a lifesaver! When my punching tic was at its worst, I almost broke my knuckle – that's when I bought myself a pair of gloves.

The ones that actually work the best are fingerless gloves made for motorcyclists. They don't restrict hand movement at all so I can still get on with daily tasks, and there's a hard covering over my knuckles. So when I punched the wall, it would hurt the wall more than it hurt me! If this sounds like something that could help you, both the helmet and the gloves can be purchased on Amazon.

Many of us with TS have some sort of motor tic involving our neck. It's an extremely common tic, and I've never actually seen someone with Tourette's who doesn't have some kind of neck twitch. If our neck tics are bad, it can cause muscle pain. There are two aids for this which have both been successful for me. Neck pillows, like the travel ones that fit around your neck, can work really well if you fling your head back like me. It stops my head from going back too far and also prevents whiplash.

Then there's one of my favourites: heat pads. These can be so soothing. I have a long rectangular one that's filled with beads and lavender, so not only is the warmth comforting, the smell is so lovely too. I heat it in the microwave for sixty seconds, then place it round my neck and it's like a warm hug!

Fidget toys are great for anyone with any type of tics at all. Or if you have anxiety, ADHD or autism, for example. They can keep our hands busy and our minds distracted. There are so many different types out there too. Some are larger, which is still great, but if you want something more discreet for out in public, there are smaller ones available as well. One of my favourites is called a 'fidget ring'. It's so great for fiddly fingers and it's really subtle too.

I always make sure I have a fidget toy in my pocket or my bag when I leave the house. It's so helpful to keep my hands busy because sometimes if I have nothing in my hands, my tics make me hit things, other people or myself.

I have a biting tic which makes me bite my hands, other people, or even just random objects! It can be painful and unhygienic. Then I discovered chewelry! Necklaces that have a pendant made from silicone, designed specially for biting. It takes a little while to feel comfortable using it, but if I feel that tic, the urge to bite something, I just bite the necklace and it stops me from biting into my skin. They are also used for children with sensory difficulties.

Showering with Tourette's isn't an easy task. For some reason my tics compete with the noise of the shower to see who's the loudest! So when I'm in the shower I shout, yell and often bang on the walls. It can be frustrating because all I want to do is wash my hair! So now I have music playing loudly from my phone every single time I shower. It makes a world of difference. So if you have TS and struggle with showering, give it a try.

I also have a shower stool, which is a small stool that you place in the shower so that you can wash your hair and shower sitting down rather than standing up. I mostly use this in case of a seizure in the shower, but it helps with my leg-drop tics a lot and keeps me safe.

Music is amazing therapy, and helps me even when I'm out and about. Shopping with TS can be a big trigger for a lot of us. If I know I'm going to a big shop I take my headphones. This means that if I get too anxious and my tics get worse, I listen to music through my headphones and it helps so much.

Due to our motor tics, some of us have broken phones and other electronics. I have a phone case with silicone corners, so now if I drop it or throw it, my phone just bounces and doesn't cause any damage. If you type online 'heavy duty phone case' and search for your type of phone you can find some great ones.

I think that covers all things practical! Now I'd love to share with you some important lessons I've learnt so far in my journey with TS. I know there will be more to come, and hopefully we can discover those together.

# Some Things I Want Others with TS to Know

- Just because you may not get visible injuries from your tics it doesn't mean your case isn't valid.
- If people stare at you, so what? Smile at them and show them you're not scary!
- Own your disability – yeah, you've got Tourette's, strut your stuff!
- Celebrate the achievements – you ate a meal without getting food everywhere? That's amazing!
- Don't feel like you have to suppress – if you're around people who wouldn't accept you for ticcing, that's nothing to do with you. It shows you what kind of a person they are.
- Educate! Teach people about your condition. The more people understand, the more they accept.
- No, you don't look ugly when you tic.
- Don't feel guilty for not ticcing. We've all been there; we are relaxed and our tics are calm, yet somehow we feel like we should be ticcing. You're not faking – don't turn the positives into a negative!
- If your tics physically hurt someone, it's not your fault.
- Severe or mild, you're still part of the Tourette's community and you are valid.
- It's okay to have rest days – we move A LOT so it's no wonder we get tired. Allow yourself to get your energy levels back up.
- Don't compare your case of Tourette's to someone else's.

- It took me a while to feel confident about my disability – don't worry if you're not there yet. You will get there; it just takes time and a bit of self-lovin'!

# What the Tourette's Community Would Like You to Know

I know approaching someone to talk about their disability can feel incredibly daunting, and sometimes rude, but I also know you may still have questions about what it's really like to live with Tourette's syndrome. To get as many answers as possible, I have spoken to other individuals with TS about what they would most like you to know.

'I think the most important thing I've found out about living with TS is that we don't all tic the same way, there's complex tics like sometimes my tics rhyme and make tuneful songs. Also, just because we have TS it doesn't make us any less than everyone else. We are just as capable and probably twice as strong.'

'I feel like one of the hardest parts of having Tourette's is other people's judgement and expectations. If more neurotypical/able-bodied people stood up for us then that would make our lives quite a bit easier at least.'

'All tics are valid. Whether it's Tourette's, motor tic disorder, anxiety tics or any other tic disorder, they can all be debilitating and all sufferers should be respected no matter what. And there should be adjustments made in education and work places to accommodate them if they need it.'
'Just because you catch me on a good tic day, it doesn't mean I'm faking or I don't have Tourette's! Tics can wax and wane and we can go through really good spells, the same way we can go through bad spells.'

'It can be hard to even sleep without medication because of the severity of some of our tics. It's frustrating, I would love to go just one day without tics, I'd be so grateful.'

'I want people to know that it may seem like a good tic day to outsiders, but there are so many tics that people can't see.'

'A lot of things are affected by our tics. Sometimes we lose independence and cannot drive or bathe alone, or go for walks alone as we might hurt ourselves – it's not something we can just ignore or get on with our lives with.'

'When the tics or tic attacks stop for a while, they're still affecting us. We are exhausted and need time to recover. It can be hard to focus or pay attention. For you it's just the tics, for us it's the side-effects as well, please be patient with us!'

Thank you to all you awesome people for sending in a quote!

Unfortunately, having a condition like TS means we experience discrimination from those who don't understand that we really can't help it. My lovely friend in New Zealand named Jade O'Connell was in an airport, about to board a flight on her way to a camp where people with Tourette's can go to relax, take part in activities and meet others like us.

Jade was told that she couldn't board the plane. She was told that she was disruptive and a danger to the crew and other passengers. Jade had informed them in advance that she had Tourette's syndrome, but the staff claimed they hadn't been notified. Jade actually missed a day of Tourette's camp because of this and it's totally unacceptable and unfair. No one should be treated this way.

Since then, another girl in New Zealand, also with TS, has experienced the exact same discrimination. She was stopped by the captain from boarding the flight after hearing her tic. She was anxious that day and hadn't slept very well so her tics were worse. She was repeating one particular tic which caught their attention. She was saying, 'I've got a gun.' Despite explaining that she had Tourette's, and that she couldn't control it, she too was denied travel because of her tics.

We understand that sometimes the things we say are socially unacceptable, but our brain says them because it knows we shouldn't. We hate saying them just as much as you dislike hearing them – in fact, even more so.

Instead of facing discrimination because of something out of our control we should be treated with respect. I have that same tic; I have said it in public before and it's awful. It's the last thing I want to be saying. Yet I know that I simply cannot help it and other people should understand that too.

Incidents like this remind me why I do what I do on my

social media. If bringing awareness and increased knowledge about this condition means that I can stop people experiencing such treatment then that's a job well done! My aim is to create a more understanding society, so that those who have disabilities or differences don't have to be afraid to just live their lives.

# What an Experience...

Okay, time to get mushy for a bit.

*Important moment of self-love to reflect and feel so proud of myself.*

It still hasn't quite sunk in that I've written a book. I think it's going to take a while! Going through such awful things but coming out the other side and writing it all down to inspire others ... I did that!!

Writing this book has been an incredible experience, it has been my therapy. I wrote this during the third lockdown, and, thanks to Covid, I haven't seen Liz, my therapist, in almost a year. So this book has been my therapist!

Having the opportunity to share my experiences with the world to hopefully help other people really is a blessing.

Writing a book when you have disabilities is a lot harder than for the average author. There were so many ups and downs that I didn't even think of when I accepted the amazing offer to write a book, such as my tics slamming the keyboard and typing in random letters. I had days where my FND flared up and my hands locked up in a ball so I couldn't do any typing. This stressed me out a lot because I had so much I still needed to write, especially when it got closer to the deadline! The whole day I spent paralysed from the neck down was so awful; I couldn't work on my book at all, I couldn't even feed myself. Thankfully the next day it had almost fully passed so as soon as I could I was back to typing at my desk.

Keeping this book secret for the first five months was a nightmare too! My tics would shout, 'I'm writing a book!!' which of course is not ideal. When I finally announced it to everyone, I felt this huge weight off my chest.

A massive thank-you to the wonderful Little, Brown Books who made this possible, and the lovely people I have worked with along the way. You have all been so helpful and so understanding when I've had flare-ups, and just generally really awesome!

Lots of love to all the people who allowed me to mention them in this book, especially those who sent in a piece of writing for me; your words have been so lovely.

I hope this book has made you smile or benefited you in some way. If you are struggling with any of the issues I've talked about, please reach out or talk to someone you trust. I'm proud of you.

If like me you haven't done too well at school, maybe you failed a couple exams (I absolutely did that), I'm hoping I have shown you that it's not the end of the world. I was rubbish at school. Academically, it's just not for me. I failed maths terribly, all the sciences and a couple other subjects too. I simply couldn't get the hang of it.

Yet look at me now. Publishing a book, selling my art all over the world even though my art teacher brought me down so much, and doing so many great things. I wish I'd known/believed when I was fourteen/fifteen that passing your exams isn't everything. You can still achieve so much.

Having severe Tourette's that took away my dream of being a teaching assistant and has affected me so badly has been heartbreaking. It's been really hard to adjust to the change. Although it wasn't sudden and my health slowly deteriorated over the years, I never thought I would be like this. Every day with my disorders is so unpredictable, but that doesn't mean I can't be happy and successful!

This book has made it all worth it. A little bit at least! Being able to share my daily struggles with the world is incredible. Receiving messages from supporters who tell me that what I do has made an impact, even from parents thanking me, just lifts me up in a way I can't explain. It is an honour to have this platform and this book to be able to educate so many.

Thank you so much for reading, take care of yourselves,
Evie Meg xx

P.S. Harvey wanted to choose the very last word in this book and I can't let him down. Weetabix.